D0354136

E^4

Evaluating, Entering, Enhancing, & Exiting

PRIVATELY OWNED BUSINESSES

Advocates
Press

Printed in the United States of America

FIRST EDITION

Library of Congress Cataloging-in-Publication Data

Bumstead, William (Bill)
        E4 / William (Bill) Bumstead. – 1st ed.
p. cm.
ISBN 1-930899-16-5
LCCN 2002109159

DESIGN BY JEFF STANTON

Published by Contrary Creek Publishers

DEDICATION

This volume is dedicated to the business owners across America who were affected by the horrendous tragedy that occurred in New York and Washington D.C. on September 11, 2001. The cowards who committed these terrorist attacks have no appreciation or understanding for those individuals who live the American dream of owning their own business.

This book serves as a reminder that the strength of these American businesses who suffered loss of life and financial hardship, always rise again and stand together to continue the American Dream of Business Ownership.

ABOUT THE AUTHOR

William W. (Bill) Bumstead
PBC, FCBI, CBC, BCB, LPI, LREB, SBA, BEC, MEA

In addition to assisting entrepreneurs in Evaluating, Entering, Enhancing and Exiting business ownership, Mr. Bumstead has spent over three decades training other professionals in the Mergers & Acquisitions industry. His accomplishments have included two college degrees, a Series 7 NASD Securities License, and a Series 63 Texas Securities License. He has also earned a real estate broker license in Colorado and Texas.

He has served as President of local, and state chapters of industry professional associations, as well as being honored as "Professional of the Year" by his home chapter. He has served on the Boards of Director of several industry associations at all levels. His professional certifications include:

PBC: Primary Business Consultant
FCBI: Certified Business Intermediary and a Fellow of the National Association
CBC: Certified Business Counselor
BCB: Board Certified Broker
LPI: Licensed Private Investigator
LREB: Licensed Real Estate Broker
SBA: Senior Business Analyst
BEC: Business Enhancement Consultant
MEA: Machinery & Equipment Analyst

Mr. Bumstead is the author of over fifteen books and training manuals used in the industry and articles in state and national publications. He is also a widely used speaker and trainer. He resides in Trinidad, Colorado, with his wife Maria.

ACKNOWLEDGMENTS

One of America's more successful Primary Business Consultants recently made the comment that "None of us are as smart as all of us," and I enthusiastically agree! Consequently, in these pages I have enlisted the opinions and comments of some of the more successful street warriors in the industry. They are providing un-compromising advocacy for entrepreneurs who are Evaluating, Entering, Enhancing and Exiting business ownership all across America.

Their experience and savvy counsel have made these chapters more street-worthy to those who deal daily with the challenges of operating and ultimately receiving their just rewards in retirement from businesses. They have provided invaluable innovation and review. Many thanks to the following for their contributions:

George D. Abraham, CBC, FCBI, BCB, BCBA, AAR, CFEA

Maria Bumstead, PBC, SBA, BEC, LREB, MEA

Angela K. Bumstead, DC

Mike Bruce, PBC

Joe Camp, PBC, CBC, SBA, BEC, MEA

Matt Donnelly, PBC, CBC, CBOA, BEC, CREA

Glenn Fitzgerald, PBC, SBA, BEC, MEA

Carol Godsey, PBC

Don Godsey, PBC

Frank Gutta, PBC, CPA

Kenneth R. Hughes, PBC, CBC, SBA, LREB

James R. Imrie, PBC, CBC, SBA, BEC

Jay Knoblett, PBC, CBC, SBA, BEC, MEA

Gregory J. Koutoulas, CPA

Bob McGinty, PBC, CBC, SBA, BEC, MEA

Diana Merced, PBC, SBA, BEC, MEA

Peter Nemkov, Attorney at Law

Randall Oestreicher, PBC, CBC, Ph.D.

Alan J. Statz, PBC, SBA, BEC, MEA

Norman Mott Williamson, PBC, CPA, CFP

Many thanks to all,

William W. (Bill) Bumstead
PBC, CBC, FCBI, BCB, SBA, BEC, LREB, LPI, MEA

FOREWORD
Shannon P. Pratt, DBA, CFA, FASA, MCBA, CM&AA

Those who are contemplating Entering business owner-ship or already own a business will benefit from this book. The author draws on over 30 years of experience to give the reader his tips and personal views on purchasing, operating, and selling a business.

The author advocates using advisors (for valuation and other purposes) who are independent.

He puts a great deal of emphasis on value, and properly so. Even an excellent business is not attractive if you cannot Enter it for a price that allows you a market rate of return on your investment. Throughout ownership, he stresses building the value of the business. When Exiting, it is frustrating to set a price that the market will not bear and then sit on the business hoping that some fool will come along and pay it. (Happily, most good business consultants now will not accept a listing at a price above what they believe the business can justify.)

He gives a very clear and concise list of steps to take when contemplating Entering an existing business. He discusses advantages and disadvantages of various forms of business ownership, including sole proprietorships, general partner-ships, limited partnerships, C corporations, S corporations, and other forms of entities. He advocates that partnerships always have a written agreement, because partnerships always end (no one is immortal). He also discusses Employee Stock Ownership Plans (ESOPs) and their advantages for Entering or Exiting a business.

His chapter on financing for the business is very straight-forward and easily readable, yet it covers all the major bases. It addresses down payments, buyer's notes to seller, and bank financing, which includes SBA guaranteed financing.

He also presents an insightful chapter on obstacles to

transferring business ownership and how to overcome them.

Finally, he has a lengthy and excellent chapter on Common Mistakes. While his experience shows through in many chapters, nowhere are his observations presented as keenly as in this chapter. <u>Just avoiding one of the common mistakes is worth the price of the book.</u>

Shannon P. Pratt, DBA, CFA, FASA, MCBA, CM&AA
Willamette Management Associates
Business Valuation Resources
Portland, Oregon

TABLE OF CONTENTS

INTRODUCTION

No man needs sympathy because he has to work...
Far and away the best prize that life offers is the
chance to work hard at work worth doing.
Theodore Roosevelt, Labor Day Address, 1903

The entrepreneur's dream of owning his/her own business and ultimately reaping the rewards of a profitable Exit is still very alive and well! In fact, it has never been better since we first became involved in mergers and acquisitions over three decades ago. We have large numbers of healthy businesses, which are being pursued by aggressive entrepreneurs. This combination makes a very vibrant marketplace not only for those Exiting business ownership, but also for those Entering business ownership.

This volume is intended to help you achieve the greatest profits and other rewards possible during each phase of Evaluating, Entering, Enhancing and Exiting business ownership. Another title for this book could have been a "Long-Term Common Sense Approach to Appraising, Buying, Improving and Selling Businesses." We feel, however, that buying and selling are really not the best terms because there are many more ways to Enter and Exit business ownership than just buying and selling. You may find other options better for you. Consequently, we'll use the terms "Entering" and "Exiting" business ownership. We will additionally use the terms "Evaluating" and "Enhancing" to represent the appraising and improving phases in the entire cycle of business ownership. Please notice that we have used the acrostic of four E's to help you trace the phases through the book.

In these pages, entrepreneurs and their advisors will find assistance in beginning the process by Entering better businesses through a more appropriate Evaluation process.

Techniques are provided for Enhancing production, profits and enjoyment during ownership. You'll also find industry secrets to make the final Exiting strategy so rewarding that you'll enjoy the golden years of retirement with more financial security.

Success in business ownership doesn't happen by accident or come as the result of compromising advice. Achieving your goals are your birthright, but obviously not guaranteed. It is the result of hard work, strategic planning, un-compromising counsel and living in a business friendly society.

Hopefully, you have found this book in the early phases of your career and ideally before you Enter business ownership. This will give you the advantage of understanding the proper concept of each phase and gain a better appreciation of the requirements of all issues and parties involved.

In Entering and Exiting negotiations, each side needs to understand the logic of the other's point of view, which can be peppered with un-compromising counsel. This does not dilute your strategies. Rather, it better prepares you to accomplish your individual goals. From the standpoint of time and expense, we hope to minimize your investments while maximizing your rewards. You need to know what to expect in each of the four phases of the complete ownership cycle. This will allow you to be in a controlling posture instead of a reactive one. It will smooth out the emotional roller coaster during negotiations and minimize the counter productive "us against them" mind set. We live in an ever-changing market where much more can be accomplished with better informed participants.

Ultimately, all parties should seek to reach fair agreements to produce a win-win for everyone through all four ownership phases. With the advantage of strategic Evaluation and Enhancement, today's Entering entrepreneur will become tomorrow's Exiting success. Actually, one becomes the mirror

2

image of the other. These chapters will fill your educational gaps and prepare you for improved long-term achievements.

If, however, you have already Entered ownership, or, are possibly considering an Exit strategy, these leading edge concepts will serve you well. You can enjoy greater profits from meeting your challenges well informed and aggressively pursuing your dreams. As professionals in the industry, we find ourselves more often initially involved with owners considering or already implementing their Exit strategy. If you are at this point and missed out on the advantages of securing this information earlier, it is even more important that you now sharpen your focus and make these last days of ownership pay off handsomely for you. You cannot afford to miss a single beat at this phase. Lost dollars are like lost sleep, you never get them back...so, don't lose any more!

Common sense, results oriented entrepreneurs should always seek qualified help in each of the four phases. The important need of choosing adequately trained, certified and un-compromising advisors to be your aggressive advocates for the long-term will make it easier as you approach each phase from a very different and more profitable perspective.

Hopefully, you will read this book from cover to cover and utilize these concepts in all four phases of your business ownership cycle. Realistically, we understand that some will find their favorite or most needed chapters from the Table of Contents and read them first. It is with this in mind that we have written each concept as a stand-alone chapter. Please understand that this will cause some repetition among the chapters.

Fasten your seat belt and get ready for an Enhanced ride through each phase of your career. You will achieve better production, profits and enjoyment as you Evaluate, Enter, Enhance and Exit the entrepreneur's dream of business ownership!

BUSINESS OWNERSHIP CYCLE

PRIMARY BUSINESS CONSULTANTS
Coach The Entrepreneur Through All Phases!

LONG TERM ADVOCACY FOR INDEPENDENT BUSINESS OWNERS

It is one of the most beautiful compensations
of this life that no man can sincerely try to
help another without helping himself.
Ralph Waldo Emerson

After Ralph Nader graduated from law school, he created a lifetime position for himself in society by taking on large corporations and becoming America's Consumer Advocate. Prior to Naders' Consumer Advocacy, there was not as much of this type of movement. At this writing, there are now Consumer Advocates in almost every major metropolitan area. From radio talk show hosts and television personalities to government agencies, everyone is attempting to take their piece of flesh from independent business owners as well as the large corporations.

It is time someone took a stand for the business owner who gives a lifetime of talent and resources serving the public in order to earn a decent return on their investment. Some begin with meager resources and sacrifice for years providing for their families and building for retirement. Help is available to assist the business owner increase performance and profits during ownership, as well as increase and protect their ultimate value for retirement. America's business advocates are known as *Primary Business Consultants* providing counsel in every phase of the business ownership cycle. Not only do these professionals provide assistance in building financial security, they assist in reducing the stress of business ownership and increase the benefits of enjoyment, credibility and respect in the business community!

The individual owner of every business will sooner or later

Exit that business and someone else will Enter the ownership. The sooner each party begins preparations for that event, the more rewarding it will be for all concerned. Ideally, an Exit strategy should be developed from the day one Enters the business and become a part of every major decision made during the ownership cycle. Consequently, whether you plan to reap the highest rewards in an Exit plan for your golden years or Enter ownership, you must also commit to invest in a constant program of Enhancement that can be measured to increase production and profits on a consistent basis. This sounds simple and surely you agree it is a worthy objective. If this were indeed so simple, why is it that so many independently owned businesses ultimately sell for significantly less than could have otherwise been achieved, or worse yet, never sell at all?

Many independent business owners choose to start or Enter a business around what they do best, which is why they excel and achieve real success. However, Entering right, planning for and achieving the highest value in their ultimate Exit of that business is often not part of what they do best. This is why most will eventually seek help, as indeed they should. Many wait too long to seek help. Some unfortunately receive uncoordinated and compromised advice from self-serving professionals. More than a few make the potential costly mistakes of trying to go it alone or operating by the seat of the pants...obviously without much forethought.

In addition to waiting too long to initiate and implement long term plans, some owners also ignore the common thread of using independent third parties which runs through all important decisions in life. Fortunately, many who are honest about their strengths and weaknesses are smart enough to realize they do not excel in all areas. Therefore, they seek the best available third-party professional advice in issues outside their expertise. Experience has taught us that when we need medical, legal, accounting and other types of specialized assistance, we seek highly trained specialists. Hopefully, we will also seek this third-party type of counsel in our business decisions early enough to allow for preventative measures and meaningful Enhancements instead of just reacting to emergencies.

Entering and Enhancing ownership properly can produce a bigger pot of gold at the end of the rainbow. You cannot have one without the other. To think and act otherwise can be disastrous. Some go through their entire ownership cycle never realizing that the same eight (or eighteen) hours a day could have produced much more of everything.

What every business owner needs from the beginning to the end is an un-compromising advocate who will coach them through the planning and achievement of the maximum financial and intangible benefits of the American Dream of business ownership. This professional must plan for and protect the interests of the entrepreneur owner above all other interests. He/she must lead you to Enter business ownership right, Enhance production, profits and value to ultimately Exit ownership for more! They should become the *Primary Business Consultant* to whom you turn during any event that effects these four phases.

He/she helps the entrepreneur owner manage multiple events and professional providers over the long term. As a result, the entrepreneur owner retains control of his/her destiny and avoids unnecessary costs and confusion arising from conflicts of interest among competing issues and professionals. With a long-term perspective, this primary coach will hold the focus on increased profits and other positive changes that increase the ultimate value of the business. Periodic services from other specialists will be needed on the team. Without them, ultimate success would be compromised. However, it becomes more likely that the ball will be carried across the goal line more successfully when there is a coach capable of wisely coordinating the talents of all involved.

This coach is a consistent advocate, protecting the highest interest of the independent business owner as he/she Evaluates, Enters, Enhances and ultimately Exits business ownership. *Primary Business Consultants* can coordinate all of these phases. Their value will be most beneficial when allowed to coordinate the entire business ownership experience. He/she will provide the important common thread of un-compromised advocacy for your entire cycle. This allows owners to enjoy the highest achievable rewards during each phase of the process. Without one, an owner could seriously compromise his/her final retirement potential, as well as income and enjoyment in the ownership process.

Almost every major social or economic group in the world enjoys the protection of an advocate. Women, children, consumers, the poor and many others have advocates who champion their cause. To whom can the business owner turn for advocacy for the long term? This should be a professional with un-compromising concern for accomplishing better decisions over an entire career.

How does an entrepreneur choose this professional that we call the *Primary Business Consultant*? First, this professional must be properly trained and have experience in all four of the E's, not just one or a few of them. Check their training and credentials. A person advising you in the Entering or Exiting of business ownership should have an accreditation such as the PBC (*Primary Business Consultant*), etc. In helping you prepare for Evaluating and securing an appraisal, the SBA (Senior Business Analyst) is appropriate. The BEC (Business Enhancement Consultant) prepares a professional for participation in business Enhancement and start-up activities. Obviously, there are other credentials, which train professionals for each specific performance.

Undoubtedly, you have noticed that we have used the terms un-compromising and un-compromised in our characterization of this professional. This professional must seek your best interest in their counsel and actions just like all other un-compromised professionals. For instance, your primary care doctor treats you individually with concern for your specific needs. After appropriate diagnostic tests, he prescribes treatments individualized for you. Your accountant prepares your individual tax return with emphasis on results that will maximize your financial interests. Your attorney is your advocate who fights aggressively for your interests.

Most importantly, no un-compromised professional will promise you something for nothing. Anyone who does otherwise has just told you the first lie, with more lies to follow. If a doctor tells you to get a blood test, you get it and you pay for it. If he/she prescribes medication or treatment, you get it, pay for it and follow through. To expect a physician to pay for these for you would be to place him/her in a potential compromising position, allowing them to prescribe only that which they could personally afford, or in which they might have a personal interest. Other un-compromising professionals act accordingly. This type of performance is not only required by their professional ethics, it is the best test of their concern for your interest above their own.

Evaluating, Entering, Enhancing and Exiting business ownership can be among the most important decisions of your life. In selecting the professionals you rely upon, the cheapest may not always be the best. An entrepreneur should consider this as important as heart surgery, and it's not time to look for a discount surgeon. The better results of your business decisions will be remembered long after you've forgotten the cost. Discounters never add quality or value to anything. The selection of a *Primary Business Consultant* is no exception. Better services can be provided only when the professional continues to invest a portion of his/her profits in continuing education. The best ones must charge fees that allow for these necessary improvements. The more they do for themselves, the more they can do for you. The additional results you receive should be in multiples of what you pay properly chosen professionals!

To be sure you have an un-compromising advocate for a *Primary Business Consultant*, you put them to the same tests of professional ethics as others you use. When a professional offers to help you Evaluate, Enter, Enhance or Exit a business without expecting your financial participation in the process, they have just told you that first lie. Very likely you would be placing yourself at risk of having them suggest actions that would be limited by their personal financial limitations. Motivated by their own personal financial circumstances, such providers might try to talk you into a transaction just so they can achieve a quick commission. They might also just simply put you in a pool of other clients, which they treat as a group, rather than individually. This would put you in what we call a Las Vegas Gamble. We all know that while some win big in Vegas, the overwhelming majority lose. You should insist that they treat you individually and report to you on a regular basis regarding actions taken, resources expended and the results of each. In order to receive this un-compromised individual treatment, you must be willing to personally support these actions financially, and follow through just like with your doctor.

You must also test their professional ethics regarding their genuine concern for clients first, above their personal interests. Every business and each client is dramatically different. All entrepreneurs cannot be treated the same. A *Primary Business Consultant* should be like a primary physician. The true professional must be willing to put aside their ego and call in a third-party when appropriate. Consistently pursuing the ultimate best results for the client is the test of the true professional.

11

History contains many examples of how genuine concern for the other person ultimately produces rewards for all concerned.

Consider the true story of a Scottish farmer named Fleming who was working on his farm trying to provide a modest living for his family. He heard a cry for help coming from a dangerous bog nearby. He immediately dropped his tools and ran toward the frantic cries.

There he found a boy stuck up to his waist in black muck. The youngster was obviously terrified, screaming and struggling to free himself. Without any concern for his own safety, farmer Fleming waded in to save him from what could have been a slow, terrible death.

The next day, a fancy carriage pulled up to the farmer's modest home. A well-dressed nobleman stepped out and introduced himself as the father of the boy whom the farmer had saved. "I want to show my gratitude and appreciation for what you did for my son. Please let me pay for the best education available for your son. For, if he is anything like his father, it will be a great investment."

Reluctantly, Fleming agreed.

His son grew up to graduate from St. Mary's Hospital Medical School in London, and later went on to discover penicillin. It was penicillin that later saved the life of the same nobleman's son from pneumonia.

Sir Winston Churchill was the name of the nobleman's son saved twice by farmer Fleming's family. England fondly remembers the many un-compromising heroic deeds Sir Winston performed for his country. Had anyone compromised in any of these circumstances, none of these wonderful accomplishments would have been possible!

In addition to the several value-added services available from your *Primary Business Consultant*, be sure you select someone who will not be involved in any compromising position with your future. Make sure you achieve a relationship with him/her that guarantees a genuine concern for your interests, first. These characteristics will produce a win-win for both you and the professional.

To avoid the use of imitators, you may ask to see a copy of their official certification of training as a *Primary Business Consultant*. Choose the right one today and stay with him/her for the long-term!

BUSINESS OWNERSHIP CYCLE

PRIMARY BUSINESS CONSULTANTS
Coach The Entrepreneur Through All Phases!

EVALUATING BUSINESS OWNERSHIP

The more that is left to chance,
the less chance there is for success.
Unknown Author

Entering, Enhancing, and Exiting entrepreneurs have in common at least one very important need. This is the need for an independent, third-party appraisal to determine the real value of a business. Those Entering business ownership are concerned that the price they pay is not too high. Exiting business owners are sensitive to the possibility of leaving money on the table with a price that is too low. Enhancing entrepreneurs need to monitor the value of their business on a regular basis to be sure the value is growing appropriately.

It would be devastating for an Exiting business owner to find out after a transaction is consummated that they agreed to a price that was too low. This often happens when they do not secure an independent appraisal before they put the business on the market, thus allowing the Entering prospect to be the only one securing an appraisal. If an Entering prospect allows the Exiting business owner to be the only one with an appraisal, they run the risk of being forced into a higher price because they did not secure an appraisal in their own interest. There is also a risk to the Entering prospect if they allow the financial institution providing the loan to be the only party with an appraisal. They may be seduced into a lower loan value. The reality is that all parties to a buy-sell business ownership transaction should secure their own independent third-party appraisal...both the Exiting and Entering parties, as well as the financing institution. This allows the Exiting party to protect their hard earned value. The Entering prospect can be sure they do not pay too much and the bank is assured of adequate equity to protect their loan. Business owners should always be concerned that the potential sales value of their business grows on a continuing basis. We call them Enhancing business owners because they constantly seek ways to Enhance their business value for an ultimate Exit strategy. In fact, businesses owned under an ESOP (Employee Stock Option Plan) are required by law to secure an independent third-party appraisal on an annual basis. Many corporate charters require an annual appraisal in order to protect the value of the shares owned by investors. Regardless of the type of ownership, we recommend a third-party appraisal on an annual basis!

Sooner or later, every business owner will Exit their business which will be Entered by another entity. We are obviously suggesting that both entities secure their own independent appraisal to *protect* their own interest. If part of the transaction is to be financed by any federal regulated institution, that institution will require the appraisal. At this writing, they are requiring two separate appraisals in some instances.

The appraiser(s) should be an independent third-party who has no other business relations with the party for whom they are performing the appraisal. A respected professional will not violate this ethic because they are concerned first for their client. Another party to a transaction would be justified in questioning the validity of an appraisal performed by an accountant, attorney, consultant or other professional who has, or is, representing a party in the current transaction.

Some Exiting business owners have experienced as much as a 10-30% loss when not using an independent third-party appraisal. The same result can be true for an Entering party to a transaction. Another benefit gained from the use of independent third-party appraisals in a buy-sell transaction is the opportunity to gain control over the negotiations. Unfortunately, it is estimated that in over 75% of buy-sell transactions, many of the parties involved do not secure their own independent appraisal. Consequently, the one(s) with an appraisal has leverage over those who do not.

Appraisals, valuations or evaluations? A frustrating aspect of the mergers and acquisitions industry is the inconsistency of terminology. One of the most misunderstood areas of terminology are terms used to refer to the process of placing a market value on a business or professional practice. Some call this process *appraisal*, while others call it *valuation* or *evaluation*. For over 20 years we have used one of the largest business appraisal firms in America and they use the term *appraisal*.

Basically, USPAP (Uniform Standards of Professional Appraisal Practice), governed by the Appraisal Foundation created by Congress, allows an appraiser to use the "departure provision" to accommodate the use of cost effective appraisals to meet the individual needs of the client. The departure provision allows the appraiser to perform appraisals (valuations, evaluations or whatever the terminology) where certain areas of the narrative report can be eliminated if they would not normally be necessary for the function of the assignment. Such departure provisions could be a verification of the books and records, a narrative of the operations and history of the company, a narrative of the industry, local and national economy, etc. In most instances, all parties would already be familiar with these areas and do not need the repetition, even though these important subjects should be researched by the appraiser.

As long as the report meets this criterion, the descriptive title of the report is not affected. However, some appraisers in order to clarify this to the public, will use terms other than appraisal. This is often a misunderstood and debated subject in the industry.

In our opinion, the terminology is not the most critical aspect. What is most important is that the report is provided by a professional not only familiar with the mechanics of appraisals, but more importantly a veteran of the industry with years of experience in the actual transfer of hundreds of businesses. For instance, in addition to authoring books and articles on the subject, producing computer software on the subject and a widely used speaker, the appraiser we use has personally served as the consultant in hundreds of consummated business transfers. What's more important is how this gives him the ability to be a winner in a courtroom should our clients ever need this expert testimony!

We insist that every client use the services of an independent third-party to deliver a report indicating the current market value of their business or professional practice, whether the terminology used is *appraisal*, *valuation*, or *evaluation*. The reports provided by the professionals we use are superior products and are as necessary to a business transfer as a blood test would be prior to heart surgery!

It's the party who comes to the table with the most *believable* appraiser that has the advantage. Actually, no one knows the exact price of your business, but everyone involved will eventually accept the opinion of the most *believable* appraiser.

Appraisal techniques are not as much a science, as they are an art. Therefore, you could secure an appraisal from three different appraisers on any one business and end up with three different market values. The report of an appraiser is no better than the information provided to him/her. This gives you an opportunity to use the services of a *Primary Business Consultant* to assist in the collection and preparation of the information given to the appraiser. *Primary Business Consultants* know the questions to be asked by an appraiser as well as the answers they like to hear. Without violating any law, moral, or ethical standard, a *Primary Business Consultant* should be allowed to gather and prepare all information to be used by your appraiser. Hence, your *Primary Business Consultant* provides the necessary "Checks and Balances" to assure everything has been accomplished to your advantage.

Now that you have chosen to use a *Primary Business Consultant* in the preparation of the information given to the appraiser, let's see how the proper selection of an appraiser gains advantage for you in *believability*. I have often heard that "there is no justice in the courtroom." Some say the winner in court is most often the one with the most believable attorney. I'm sure this is not true 100% of the time, however, it happens often enough to prove your need for choosing an appraiser with the highest *believability* factor.

In order for the appraisal results to be believed by other parties to the transaction, as well as in potential litigation, here are some issues you should consider in the selection of an appraiser:

1. Do they have general experience in the mergers & acquisitions industry?
2. How long have they been involved in the industry?
3. In how many transactions have they participated in some capacity other than an appraiser?
4. Have they held offices in organizations in the industry?
5. How many business appraisals have they performed?
6. How many business appraisals have they performed in which federal regulated institutions have provided acquisition funds?
7. What are the sizes of the largest and smallest businesses they have appraised?
8. Are they qualified to include machinery & equipment values in their appraisals?
9. Are they qualified to include environmental issues

in their appraisals?

10. What are their educational accomplishments?

11. Have they been used as an instructor in the appraisal industry?

12. Are they an author in the appraisal industry?

13. What is their accuracy record?

14. Do they own or have access to a reputable comparable database?

15. What is their record in the courtroom?

16. Does your *Primary Business Consultant* have a comfortable working relationship with the appraiser?

Beyond the fact that the lending institution will require one anyway, are there other logical and economical reasons for all parties in a buy-sell business transaction to secure an independent third-party appraisal? Yes, and here are some of them:

1. It makes all parties to the transaction informed and puts everyone on the same "page."

2. An appropriate appraisal gives that party an opportunity to influence the price from their perspective.

3. Regardless of whom you talk to, all "un-compromised" parties should suggest an independent third-party.

4. It accelerates the process and avoids stalls. With a good independent third-party appraisal in hand, negotiations with lending institutions and other parties will move quicker, and with less controversy.

5. The parties with an independent third-party appraisal of the business will enjoy more credibility and the reputation that he/she only does things right.

6. An appraisal creates a sense of urgency with less conflict.

7. The appraisal confirms the sincerity of all parties.

8. More appropriate prices are achieved with substantiated prices through an independent third-party appraisal.

9. An appraisal is not a cost…it is an investment in an appropriately priced business.
10. A good appraisal is like a good insurance policy. It produces more later than it costs now.
11. An independent third-party opinion is a common thread that runs through all important decisions of life.
12. An independent third-party appraisal reduces wasted time in the business transfer process.
13. The independent third-party appraisal removes the negative element of "chance" and allows the party with one to "control" negotiations from their perspective.
14. An appraisal from an independent third-party provides a reputation of honesty.
15. The appraisal removes the need to "compare prices."
16. Independent third-party appraisals remove the danger of "Ball Park" and "Rules of Thumb" guessing.

We are often asked, "How much should I expect to invest in the price of an appraisal?" Determining the value of your business should never be taken casually. Who you choose and how much you pay appraisers are important decisions. In a recent Associated Press article, Vivian Marino indicates the cost for an appraisal for an average small "mom and pop" business is around $10,000. Recently, we have seen prices of some appraisals run as high as $42,500. What you get and who does it for you are much more important than the price.

This is where your *Primary Business Consultant* can help you again. Remember, if you are going to court and the stakes are high, you want nothing less than the best. In securing an independent third-party appraisal, you don't have to pay the most to get the best. Your *Primary Business Consultant* knows where to go to get the best for less. Additionally, because of the respect in the industry for *Primary Business Consultants*, some of the better appraisers will suggest your *Primary Business Consultant* should do some of the local "leg work" and will discount the price accordingly. The main issue here is that you will remember the value the appraisal brings to your transaction long after you have forgotten the price of the appraisal.

After over three decades in the industry, we have heard most of the questions regarding the need for appraisals in the transfer of business ownership. Since you may face some of the same questions, we'll share some of the issues with you:

1. How long does it take?

    The time spent in the process is largely determined by how quickly you can supply the needed information. On an average, it takes four to six weeks.

2. Why do some "brokers" not require an appraisal to sell my business?

    Some "old-style brokers" do not require an appraisal because they only play the "numbers game." They simply put a large number of businesses on the market with the hope that at least some of them will sell, regardless of the price. Consequently, they do not spend time determining the proper price or needs of the business. This places both the Exiting and Entering entrepreneurs in what we call a "Las Vegas Gamble." No one will ever know how much money is lost by everyone involved.

3. "Can my accountant do the appraisal?"

    The answer is yes, however, your accountant is not an independent third-party. Therefore, others involved in negotiations will automatically discount an appraisal price from your accountant. You could lose more in negotiations than it would have cost to use the services of an independent third-party appraiser.

4. "Can't I just let the bank pay for it?"

    Lending institutions will normally charge you for the price of the appraisal.

5. "What happens if I don't get the price I want?"

As in all important decisions in life, you want the truth, even if it hurts! Don't waste many hours and dollars trying to accomplish something that is impossible. If the appraisal is suggesting a price you can't accept, your *Primary Business Consultant* can help you correct the problems and Enhance the value of your business.

6. "I know what I want the price to be and I'm not negotiable."
   Really now, we don't make important decisions in life with our eyes closed. Even if you receive bad news, it's not the end of the world. Your *Primary Business Consultant* can help you Enhance negative challenges.

7. "Why must I pay for the appraisal before I know the results?"
   Appraisal societies require that appraisers be paid before they begin work. This keeps them from being tempted to "alter the results" in order to get paid.

8. "Aren't there computer programs out there that you could use to value my business?"
   Yes, there are, however, appraisal computer programs are no better than the person using them. This is dangerous and can cost you many multiples of what it would cost for the appropriate independent third-party appraiser.

9. "Is the cost of the appraisal based on the value of my business?"
   Definitely not! Appraisal prices are based on the anticipated amount of time and resources necessary to do the work.

10. "Can't we just use an industry "rule of thumb?"
    Rules of thumb are only one limited way to look at the price of a business. There are many other more important ingredients of a proper appraisal. To ignore the other ingredients can cost you severely in the price

of the business.

11. "Another professional in town is offering appraisals at discount prices."

    This reminds me of a billboard I recently saw on the freeway:

    A Lot of Dealerships Sell Lexus, Some Even Cheaper. It's Who You Buy One From that Makes the Ultimate Difference!

    Your independent third-party appraiser and *Primary Business Consultant* must work together (with other professionals) as a team for you. The appraiser will build his appraisal from information gathered correctly and presented properly by your *Primary Business Consultant*. This team work can make more of a difference in the price of the business than the difference in price of the appraisal you could secure from any discounter. Like a Lexus, who you get it from is an important part of the decision.

12. "I want to also sell my building and I have a lot of machinery and equipment. Who do we get to determine these prices?"

    This is another value of allowing your *Primary Business Consultant* to coordinate all of the issues. He/she will be able to secure all of these professionals at appropriate prices and "coach" the entire team to your advantage.

13. "This sounds like you are trying to sell me an appraisal."

    Frankly, no one is trying to sell you anything. Like your "primary" physician, your *Primary Business Consultant* will advise only what is best for your end result. You're not buying anything…you are simply being advised to take the steps that lead to a significantly better end result.

No one should consider **Entering, Exiting, or Enhancing**

a business without an independent third-party appraisal, any more than they would consider major surgery without a proper diagnosis.

Choose a *Primary Business Consultant* with whom you are comfortable. Then let him/her assist you in selecting the appropriate independent third-party appraiser (and other professionals) to make a winning team for you!

BUSINESS OWNERSHIP CYCLE

The Complete Cycle of Business Ownership

$E^1 E^2$

PRIMARY BUSINESS CONSULTANTS

Coach The Entrepreneur Through All Phases!

ENTERING BUSINESS OWNERSHIP

Begin doing what you want to do now. We are not living in eternity.
We have only this moment, sparkling like a star in our hand —
and melting like a snowflake. Let us use it before it is too late.
Marie Beynon Ray

Entrepreneurs considering **Entering** business ownership were previously known "as buyers." We now refer to them as **Entering** entrepreneurs because there are many effective opportunities to become the owner of a business in addition to buying a business. Someone might inherit ownership through a family transition. Some entity may choose to merge with another entity. Others may feel it appropriate to create a corporation or partnership for the purpose of **Entering** business ownership. An ESOP may be the vehicle used to **Enter** ownership. For some, a franchise may be a good option. If someone is unable to find the appropriate business through one of these forms, they may start-up a new business venture from scratch. Obviously, there are many ways to accomplish the goal. A common way to **Enter** independent business ownership is for an entrepreneur to purchase an existing business.

There have been other unfortunate phrases assigned to these individuals and other types of **Entering** entities. Some old-style professionals who do not fully understand the total buying process have unfairly characterized **Entering** entrepreneurs with the statement " buyers are liars," thus blaming the failure of transactions on only one side of the closing table. The reality is that most transaction failures are the result of improper opportunities being offered to **Entering** partici-

28

pants. No one should Enter something that is not right for them!

Properly trained *Primary Business Consultants* can assist in Entering business ownership through a variety of ways. Some Entering entrepreneurs will not find their needs met in their initial efforts at an existing businesses in the open market. Consequently, other options should be made available. This chapter will provide insight to several alternative ways of Entering independent business ownership.

The First Priority: Entering an Existing Business Ownership.

Many consider the opportunity to purchase an established, profitable business to be the best option available. The current owner(s) have already demonstrated the need for existing products and/or services. The start-up learning curve has been passed. Loyal customers and clients are evidence of the demand and quality of what is provided for the market. Employees and providers are in place with adequate planning and production. Cash flow is established to meet credit needs as well as yield rewarding profits. The business is often ready for the next stage of growth and the current owner(s) is willing to guide you into an exciting period of expansion. New ideas and enthusiasm, possibly along with an infusion of new capital, can be just what is needed to meet the challenges of the future.

A *Primary Business Consultant* will have an inventory of quality businesses available to meet your economical and geographical requirements, as well as a match for your personal skills, strengths and interests.

Possibly, the most important ingredient of your future success is to assure that the business you Enter is appropriately priced.

You should not consider purchasing one of your most important and sizeable assets without securing an independent third-party appraisal from an experienced appraiser who values businesses on a national basis. A *Primary Business Consultant* can coordinate the appraisal process to assure that the most accurate appraisal is performed for you.

The financial institution that provides the financing will require an independent third-party appraisal. It would be unsettling to find at the last minute that you paid too much after you've already negotiated your price. You will be at a severe disadvantage if you allow the Exiting owner to be the only one to drive the price with an appraisal supported only by information he/she chooses to provide the appraiser.

We live in an era of globalization and all of us are affected by what happens elsewhere, particularly in our own country. It would be a mistake to ignore appraisal trends in other economic markets, especially if using them would be to your advantage. Consequently, you need to use an appraiser who has national/international experience. A believable appraiser must have significant experience in all types of businesses with ample data to support his/her opinions of value. It is your right to work with an appraiser whose experience, independence and work product produce immediate credibility, therefore impressing the Exiting owner and his/her advisors.

In order for the appraisal to be credible to other parties to the transaction, the appraiser must be a totally independent third-party who has no other business relations with you. Your *Primary Business Consultant* can guide you in the selection of this professional. Any time you are involved in a business transaction, you should consider the possibility that your decisions and actions may be challenged in a court of law. Therefore, choose an appraiser who can best support you in such an extreme occurrence. Your *Primary Business Consultant* will have a checklist helpful in the selection of a qualified appraiser in order for you to avoid the use of compromised professionals.

Remember, by engaging a *Primary Business Consultant* you

will have an un-compromised advocate who places your interests above all others in the transaction. As a true advocate, this professional will not allow himself/herself to be placed in a position where they may face a potential conflict of interest regarding payment for their services or how they spend their time. Advocates are paid for their time and services based on what is best for the client, not what makes it possible for them to receive the quickest commission. The fee structure of a *Primary Business Consultant* gives them the incentive to locate better businesses faster and at a significant final savings to you. This savings makes your Entering transaction easier to consummate and leaves more dollars available for the growing of your new business. The reward to the *Primary Business Consultant* is that he/she can do more transactions and earn more in the long term. This is a win-win for everyone, as is always the case when everyone is honestly motivated.

Proven methods of Entering business ownership.

In addition to purchasing an existing business, there are alternative methods of Entering business ownership. Whatever method you use, be sure you monitor the progress of the professional(s) you use. They should keep you informed of the progress through regular reports. You should approve every step and participate in and review all expenditures to help you identify better businesses sooner. Let's first discuss the purchase of an existing business.

How can you maintain confidentiality?

A *Primary Business Consultant* serves as a communications channel between those Entering and Exiting business ownership. Without this assistance and careful handling, experience suggests it is virtually impossible for these principals to maintain confidentiality in the process. He/she can open the communications process without initially revealing the identity of the principal parties, specific addresses or telephone numbers. This is definitely in your interest.

You do not want the employees finding out the business is being considered by you or they may possibly become insecure in their relationship with management and seek employment elsewhere. They might even go to work for competitors to protect the financial security of their family. You would not want them to lose interest in their work, possibly sabotage the business and/or reveal company secrets. The loss of key employees could seriously diminish the value of the business you are considering and prompt the owner(s) to react negatively to your preliminary expression of interest.

Suppliers might lose confidence in their ability to collect monies due them. They may even begin to seek other potential distribution possibilities for their products and services. This could be devastating to you. At the time of transfer you need everything to be at its best.

Bankers always become nervous when they hear anything about a business that could affect their collateral, especially the gross sales and cash flow which secure their payment. When you are considering a business purchase and third-party financing, the business needs to display the ability to grow and finance the growth.

With customers, clients and the public in general, "business as usual" should be the watchword. Nothing should be done that stimulates fear or doubt that the business will do anything less than continue to stand behind products and services delivered. In order to retain their confidence and continued business, it is essential customers and clients never hear anything to make them feel at risk!

The media is constantly in search of anything potentially sensitive or damaging. It would be bad enough if any of the above mentioned groups found out which business you were considering, and much worse if someone were to share it with newspapers, radio, television, etc. *Primary Business Consultants* will not initially reveal the identity of those Entering or Exiting business ownership until proper confidentiality documents have been signed.

A 100% guarantee of confidentiality cannot be promised, although everything should be done to try to accomplish it. There is seldom a problem when the guidelines of a *Primary Business Consultant* are followed. However, you should be additionally trained to handle your reactions should anyone else be guilty of carelessness.

What professionals do you need and when should you use them?

We are often asked if *Primary Business Consultants* are "brokers." The answer is they provide all of the services of a broker, but they are much more. They are trained to help you Enter business ownership in several ways other than just the purchase of an existing business. These professionals are certified consultants with the skills and experience to help you find a better business. Most importantly, they additionally guide you through the negotiation and closing stages, right up to the closing table where you sign the final documents and pick up the keys to your exciting future. Unlike those who only "broker" businesses in the traditional role, they go beyond and can help you in the process of Enhancing the production and profits of your new venture. This will ultimately improve the value you will receive when it is time for your own Exit strategy. Their unique structure of compensation and superior marketing strategies make them the ultimate in un-compromised client advocacy! They are then the most logical professionals to guide you through the Exit strategy. Clients consider them to be like primary family physicians. "They can deliver the baby and eventually deliver the baby of the baby."

Working in your best interest they can bring you the same

degree of professionalism that major public corporations employ a full staff of specialists to do for them. Privately owned businesses need this same quality of service, but obviously cannot afford a specialized, full-time staff. Regardless of the size of a business you Enter, you can feel comfortable that each step is handled correctly.

At the appropriate time, accountants, attorneys, tax specialists, estate planners, escrow/closing agents, appraisers, bankers and others may be needed. The *Primary Business Consultant* is the "coach" of this team and will set an example of unselfish cooperation in the coordination of all of the individual events, paperwork, activities and responsibilities of other professionals. The coach of any team normally plays a vital part in the selection of the team members. This is a necessary role because the coach often functions as a reconciliation expert to keep the process on course.

Timing is an integral part of any important event. Your coach will be a clock watcher to be sure everyone performs in a timely manner. They have dealt with most concerns many times and their professional check lists will help everyone perform at their best in a coordinated manner.

Successful teams play to the end of the game. Your *Primary Business Consultant* will help everyone understand this is your game and all involved have the responsibility to help you win it. It is always fun to be a part of a winning team. You can be confident that stress and negative aspects of professional egos will be kept to a minimum. Entering business ownership can be the next crowning event of your career and is to be enjoyed. Your team will play hard for you...your *Primary Business Consultant* will see to it! He/she is trained and ready to assist you in each step of the process.

What are the logical steps in Entering business ownership?
The initial communication with a *Primary Business*

Consultant regarding Entering an existing business can be made in a variety of ways. A properly trained *Primary Business Consultant* will be going through a marketing process for their Exiting client that involves many different steps trying to find you, the Entering entrepreneur. They want to draw your attention to appropriate business opportunities as eagerly as you want to find them. Here are a few of the things they will be doing to try to find you.

You will want to read the business opportunity ads in local, regional, national newspapers and industry publications. There you will find these professionals advertising opportunities they have available. They will be communicating with other professionals in your market area such as accountants, attorneys, insurance agents, bankers, etc., making them aware of their inventory of businesses available. They will be writing letters and making phone calls to other business owners and working their referral sources. This list of activities searching for you could include over 50 different actions. Obviously, they want to find you and will be glad to assist you in many ways.

Now that we find ourselves in generation "D" (digital), many opportunities can be found on the Internet. While the Internet has proven useful in increasing awareness of many opportunities and facilitated initial communication and the exchange of basic information, most Entering prospects need a *Primary Business Consultant* to guide them in a step by step process of due-diligence, negotiations, transaction difficulties and Enhanced growth after the purchase. We had a call recently from a client who found us on the Internet two years ago and Entered a business with our assistance. He phoned to say he was referring a friend from another state who also wanted to use our services. The Internet was obviously responsible for the first contact, but many hours of person-to-person communications followed. This is one of the values of a *Primary Business Consultant*. He/she can become your un-compromising advocate for life! Once you and a *Primary Business Consultant* have found each other, here are some steps in which you will want to be involved.

What happens when you find an existing business you like?

As soon as you have identified an existing business in which you have some interest, you will need to sign a non-disclosure document (confidentiality agreement) to protect the identity and trade secrets of the Exiting owner. Normally you will only have to do this one time because the agreement will allow you to continue to receive information on other businesses from the same *Primary Business Consultant*. This is another of the many advantages of working with one professional for the long-term.

Information can be shared with you in a variety of ways, but normally it will be provided in three basic forms. First, you should be given a "preliminary" profile on the business providing basic information. These first communications can be accomplished by telephone, fax and e-mail saving you valuable time.

If the preliminary information meets your initial criteria, you will then be given a "basic" profile, which provides more detailed information. This is normally accomplished in a face-to-face meeting with the *Primary Business Consultant*; however, fax, e-mail, telephone and mail may be appropriate where distance is a factor. In order that the professional can confirm your credible interest to the current owner of the business, you will be asked to provide "basic" information on yourself. This should include a current or recent financial history, resume and criteria important to you in seeking a business.

Assuming you have continued interest in the business, you should ask to see detailed information on the business which the *Primary Business Consultant* will have in his/her office in what is called the "master" profile of the business. With permission of the owner, you should be allowed to make copies of any information shown to you.

If you have continued interest in the business, you will obviously want to make a personal visit to the business and be involved in a period of due-diligence to verify the credibility of what has been provided to you. Ask the *Primary Business Consultant* to guide you through this process, which may involve several exercises as well as other professional advisors.

How do you Enter an existing business?

Keeping in mind that good opportunities are usually being considered by other interested parties, you will want to offer a written Letter of Intent to initiate a period in which you and the owner can agree on the basic principles of a transaction. If agreement is reached, then you will want to transition this into a binding offer to purchase. If this is your first attempt, ask the *Primary Business Consultant* to share with you examples of such forms and lead you to an attorney who can prepare documents that meet your individual needs. You may want to save on these expenses by choosing the combination of an attorney/closing agent who will legally represent your interests all the way through the closing table. In some instances, both the Entering and Exiting principals will share in the use and expenses of these legal services.

You need to share with all participating professionals the name of the *Primary Business Consultant* you have chosen to be the "coach" of the team. Be sure they understand that all procedures are to be coordinated through the *Primary Business Consultant*. He/she will want to insure that all of the necessary events take place. Here are some of them.

If you are going to use the form of a stock purchase, you will normally Enter the business ownership "as is," with the purchase of the stock, unless you negotiate otherwise. Many individually owned private businesses are Entered through the form of an asset purchase. Here you will purchase a negotiated list of assets and create your own corporation or other legal entity.

Your *Primary Business Consultant* will assist the principals of the transaction in negotiating the expense items to be prorated. You must decide how you will prorate all normal operating expenses, which may exceed twenty or more items.

You will be led through another list of items that must be completed prior to closing. This can include, among others, such things as setting the closing date, removal of contingencies, arrange for financing, counting and certifying inventory and other assets, transfer of licenses/permits, transfer of utilities, bank accounts and many other housekeeping items.

After these and other issues have been presented to the Exiting business owner, he/she will respond with an acceptance, or possibly a counteroffer. If things don't work out in a timely manner, you may need to extend your offer to purchase.

Once all parties have agreed on your offer, one of the next procedures will be to complete your due-diligence and remove all contingencies you placed in your offer. Don't forget important issues such as environmental concerns.

It is now time for the Escrow/Closing Attorney to prepare asset or stock closing documents to be confirmed by both Entering and Exiting principals. Closing documents that accurately represent the agreements of the parties will be finalized and a closing date will be set. *The Primary Business Consultant* (who has been chosen to be the "coach" of the team) will coordinate the flow of all information and communications through the closing where you will pick up your keys to your exciting future.

A potential "road map" of the entire experience of Entering an existing business is provided as follows:

1. Initial interview with a *Primary Business Consultant* regarding businesses in his/her inventory.
2. Sign a non-disclosure document to guarantee confidentiality of any information provided to you.

3. Receipt of a "Preliminary Profile" of information regarding a business in which you have interest.
4. You will be given a guide for Entering Business Ownership, which will provide you with a mini-education on Entering business ownership. You should read and fully understand this before you proceed!
5. If you have continued interest, you will be asked to provide historical financial information on yourself, a personal resume, as well as fill out a questionnaire regarding your needs, qualifications and geographical requirements.
6. Receipt of a more detailed "Basic Profile" of the business in question.
7. An opportunity to review all information available on the business which is normally contained in a "Master Profile" of the business.
8. Review of a third-party appraisal on the business.
9. A visit to the business.
10. Preparation of an offer to purchase the business to which should be attached your credit report.
11. The *Primary Business Consultant* will present your offer to the Exiting owner with an earnest money deposit.
12. Hopefully your offer will be accepted or you will receive a counter offer.
13. When your offer is accepted, your earnest money will be deposited with the Escrow/Closing Attorney.
14. You will arrange financing for the purchase.
15. There will be a period of time in which you will review the financial records of the company in an exercise called due-diligence. During this time all contingencies will be removed and/or negotiated.
16. The *Primary Business Consultant* will monitor the following activities performed by other professionals:

Title/Lien search.

Final contingency removals.

Preparation of closing documents by the Escrow/Closing Attorney.

17. The consummation of your purchase will take place at a "closing" at which time you will receive possession of your new business...Congratulations!

This is obviously a general overview of the entire process in which you will be involved in Entering the ownership of an existing business. Beyond this, you can depend on your *Primary Business Consultant* to guide you each step of the way.

If you've Entered ownership of an existing business, what's next?

After a *Primary Business Consultant* has led you to the best match of your criteria in an existing business purchase, he/she can now perform another important service for you. Although you are just starting out in a new venture, it is never too early to start realistic planning for your ultimate Exit of the business you have just Entered. Take some time to read the chapter on Enhancing business ownership to learn about the significant advantages of participating in this bold growth strategy for your business.

What happens if you do not Enter an existing business?

In the event the current inventory of businesses available does not meet your needs, another potential consideration might be to investigate franchises available through a *Primary Business Consultant.* There are advantages to purchasing a franchise. The franchisor has already solved many of the headaches you would experience in starting your own business with the concept proven by many franchises across the country. There will be a definite plan for you to follow with support from the franchisors. You can participate in national advertising that you could not otherwise afford on a limited individual budget. A *Primary Business Consultant* will often have several franchise opportunities available in your area. Ask them to share these with you and make arrangements for the franchisors to provide information for your investigation.

Should the business of your dreams not be found through the consideration of an existing business or franchise, your *Primary Business Consultant* can assist you by conducting a targeted search in the "hidden market" for a business best suited to your needs and criteria.

Speaking realistically, many Entering entrepreneurs do not find a business that meets their needs through the options already discussed. Often it just does not exist. We are told repeatedly that the search for an existing business to Enter in the "open" market has been a real education and often very frustrating. The effort forces you to look hard at your objectives, skills and financial capabilities. When all the issues have surfaced you just may not find the perfect match.

This is a good indication that you need to allow a *Primary Business Consultant* to take you into the "hidden" market for businesses that would not otherwise come to your attention. We might compare this process to what takes place in the used car market. Someone may want a 1957 Chevy two-door hard top, with a white top and blue bottom, four-inch sidewalls, and in good operating condition. This is likely not to be found advertised in any newspaper or on any used car lot. There is probably at least one in someone's garage, well protected from the elements and dangerous freeways. In order to find it, you will have to search all garages until it is found.

Many Entering entrepreneurs are looking for something that does not exist in the "open" market. If they are truly committed to finding and Entering the "right business," they should engage a *Primary Business Consultant* to conduct a professional

41

search for it. We call this a "targeted" business search because of the professional way in which it is conducted.

Several good things can happen during this exercise. If what you want exists, it will be found. If the current owner will consider an **Exit**, you'll get the business of your dreams. Ask your *Primary Business Consultant* to help you crystallize your objectives, explain the process and execute the search. At this point the *Primary Business Consultant* can now become an advocate for you, directing his/her energies not only to making the right fit, but helping you **Enter** a business with the financial objectives best suited to your needs.

Should the targeted search in the hidden market not produce the desired results, you will need to take a realistic look at your objectives and criteria. You can then change criteria, or go on to other options.

This will be the time for you to consider a new business start-up with the help of your *Primary Business Consultant*.

Now is not the time for despair. The ideal business you were not able to locate might be just what the public needs. If it does not already exist, you might possibly be on the verge of a great new venture.

With the previous experiences behind you, don't you think it would be worth investigating the feasibility of starting the business of your dreams? What you thought was bad news in the unsuccessful search for the right business, might prove to be a blessing in disguise. Over 50% of people looking for businesses find out that their ideal business does not exist in a form they want. Isn't it comforting to know that you may not be alone?

Your *Primary Business Consultant* can lead you through a "discovery" process to examine every aspect of your idea(s). You will be a vital part of this process, receiving regular reports for verification and comments.

He/she will then develop a start-up business "plan" with a specific road map to start and build your business. It is important that your *Primary Business Consultant* "monitor" the implementation of this plan on a regular basis for optimum performance, profits and ultimate future value.

If you have been through all of these steps and still haven't Entered business ownership, it's time for another re-evaluation of your criteria.

Your *Primary Business Consultant* should be affiliated with the best professionals available and can guide you in this process. You may have to adjust your thinking to what is needed, not just what you want.

A Final Thought.

We are often asked what an entrepreneur needs to be a successful business owner. Individual businesses and the persons owning them are all unique. The skills necessary for each type of business are different.

A knowledge of the industry is obviously required, but not necessarily at the beginning. What's more important is your own depth of belief in yourself and your ability to breed confidence in others. Owning a business requires you to be a leader, both with employees and clients.

An un-compromising concern for others, especially your clients, is a necessary quality for successful business ownership. Be sure you have chosen an industry in which there is a need for quality products and/or services to the public, and become the best at it.

We live in a frank and open society. You must have, or develop, the ability to handle challenges on a regular basis. Experience is a good teacher, as long as you keep it constructive.

Build around you a great "team" to support your dreams and goals. Our greatest national leaders have made their mark with the help of good advice and loyal believers. Begin this process with the selection of an appropriate *Primary Business Consultant* to guide you through all four cycles of ownership.

Finally, sooner or later you will Exit the business you have chosen. When you Enter is the ideal time to start this Exit strategy. In beginning the plans for a new home, I was recently given good advice. The advisor suggested I build it as much for the person who would buy it from me, as for my own desires. The same is true for your new business. Enhance every major decision with the thought in mind that the quality of your decisions will not only bear up your success, but will affect your ultimate reward when you Exit.

BUSINESS OWNERSHIP CYCLE

PRIMARY BUSINESS CONSULTANTS
Coach The Entrepreneur Through All Phases!

ENHANCING BUSINESS OWNERSHIP

Along the way you will stumble, and perhaps even fall;
But that, too, is normal and to be expected.
Get up, back on your feet, chastened but wiser,
And continue down the road.
Arthur Ashe

What is a Business Enhancement Plan?

A successful Business Enhancement Plan is the plan of action that accomplishes the needed objectives indicated in the independent third-party Business Enhancement Report. Your *Primary Business Consultant* will lead in the design of this plan and monitor each step in the accomplishment of increased cash flow and higher ultimate value.

This should not increase your workload because the *Primary Business Consultant* will assume the role necessary to implement the objectives. In fact, most plans will relieve you of some of your undesirable tasks and place your best talents and time in a more profitable and enjoyable role.

There will be a clear, compelling and rewarding agenda that meets the current, intermediate and ultimate goals of the owner/operator, managers, and stockholders. Meeting these challenges will significantly Enhance the growth and effectiveness of your organization. Some issues to be considered will be:

- Healthy dissatisfactions of issues that are holding you back
- A vision to guide the future
- Definition of your mission to establish principles

of success
- Goals and benchmarks to produce specific results
- Proper use of human resources
- Elimination of confusion and waste
- Better quality products and services
- Streamlined systems
- Better communications with customers and employees that will make you more distinctive
- Improved supplier relationships and profits

You will better understand how to choose a proper match between what you offer and that needed by customers and clients. Actions will be taken to create more customer loyalty, as well as how to make them call you first. Implementation of a successful Business Enhancement Plan will make the business easier to secure third party financing in your Exiting process. It puts all parties on the same page regarding the potential growth of the business. Accomplishing the goals of the plan will help you avoid leaving money on the table when you Exit. Wouldn't it be devastating to later find out you could have sold for a lot more if you had implemented a Business Enhancement Plan.

The use of a Business Enhancement Plan proves that you know what you are worth and will not accept less, which helps eliminate "low ball" offers. It is a great example that your company only does things right!

Using the Business Enhancement Plan removes the element of chance and puts you in control of your cash flow and ultimate value. It will bring purpose to those who may have lost interest and become a victim of burn out. It destroys procrastination and puts the firepower back into owners and employees alike. You will see disorganization replaced with enthusiastic organization as it brings a profitable structure to daily routines. Ask your *Primary Business Consultant* to explain the process to you!

When should a business owner consider a Business Enhancement Plan?

The business owner has one ultimate purpose… to create equity. Without this there is only one benefit available to them for the work of owning a business. That benefit is income for their own employment. There are many individuals and corporations that generate significant dollars for that employment; however when it comes time to Exit there is a rude awakening that occurs around the value of their business. That awakening is that the only thing they have is themselves and that is usually the only thing not for sale to the potential Entering prospect.

You should always be on the alert for opportunities to improve the current profits and ultimate value of your hard work and investment. How you do that is what determines whether you build equity and enhance the value or simply create more work. Our current economy rewards Enhancement now more than any period we have seen in decades. At several points every business owner will have opportunities for improvements. These may be an Exit, family succession, merger, acquisition or others. Regardless of the type of changes(s) you choose, there will be several parties wanting to participate either in purchase, employment or capital outlays if you have maximized your profits and value.

In the foregoing discussion it will be evident that a certified *Primary Business Consultant* is the best qualified to assist you. I have seen many business owners consider this option only after an appraisal has come back low or there has been a severe downturn. The beauty about this concept is that this is actually the best business practice known to man. Practiced over the long term it creates a salable vehicle or a business that can actually produce a legacy because the foundation and structure is very strong. It is never too soon to start planning your strategies. In fact, it should be a constant activity, regardless of whether you currently want to start a new business, Enter an existing business, Exit your current business or Enhance the profits and ultimate value.

This information is provided to help you understand how to Enhance the current profits and ultimate value in a way that will be ultimately rewarding for all involved. You should never allow a professional to lead you into the defeated attitude of putting your business on the market for a price less than it could be worth, when a little extra effort could produce a better price. An un-compromising *Primary Business Consultant* will be willing to suggest that you not go immediately to the market, but rather find out what it will take to improve the value. Such a reality check can produce the "best of both" results desired by everyone. Enlarge your vision and get ready for an exciting ride into a more profitable future!

The Assessment

This is the initial process in taking a snapshot of what is actually happening in the business. What we are looking for here is the actual equity in the business. Is it its product? Is it the relationships? Is it a patent, history, market share, or personnel etc? Businesses are Entered for a number of reasons in which all of the above come into play. We want to determine the current strengths in the business that give it the equity it has today. The first part of answering this question is to have an appraisal completed. How can an independent third-party business appraisal help in the Enhancement of a business? Business owners are concerned to know the value of their business for many purposes:

- Future Growth Planning
- Loan Application
- Preparation for Legal representation
- Family Succession

- Entering a Business
- Exiting a Business
- Buy-Sell Agreements
- Going Public/Private
- Preparation of a Business Enhancement Plan
- Comparison with Industry Standards
- Tax Purposes
- Estate Planning
- Divorce
- Consideration of a Merger
- Partnership Agreements
- Employee Stock Ownership Plan (ESOP)
- Compensatory Damage Issues

If your purpose involves negotiations with other entities, it would be tragic to find out at the last minute that you had based your opinions on less than appropriate values, which proved to cost you serious **money**.

You need an appraiser who has national/international experience in order to take advantage of better performance and pricing policies supported by other areas with different economies. We live in an era of globalization and are affected by what happens elsewhere. A believable appraiser must have experience in all types of businesses with comparable data to support his/her credibility. In order to be convincing to other parties, your appraiser should be a totally independent third-party who has no other business relations with you at all. You should consider that your actions might be challenged in a court of law. Therefore, you should only choose an appraiser who would best support you in such an extreme occurrence.

The second step is an on-sight full audit establishing these equities. Equities are assets the company owns that are responsible for the bottom line strength of the company. Equity is really what the Entering prospect will pay for. They have to have the perception that there is equity in what they are purchasing. Entering prospects look at this primarily in two ways. The first is Market Share otherwise known as Strategic Value. Your business can be very valuable if the strategic value is Enhanced. Secondly is the Financial Value. This value is not simply the ability to generate income. This value is a combination of free cash flow, operating systems, market share, stability etc.

Once we have established these equities we want to see what systems are in place to assure their strength and transferability (We will talk about systems shortly). Once we have established the current equities of the business we will begin to discover unearthed and partially developed equities (It is important to note we are looking for what increases the bottom line). This assessment involves the entire company including financial and production records. It usually takes 30 to 60 days depending on the size of the company. Interviews and review will be conducted with:

- Management (all levels)
- Finance
- Employees
- Selected clients
- Selected Vendors
- Attorney
- Accountant
- Banker
- Product line
- Research & Development (If present)

The information is then compiled and reviewed. You can certainly perform an audit like this on your own. What you are seeking is feedback on areas in which the company is underperforming as well as areas that are highly profitable to the company and are being compromised out of their full use. We recommend a *Primary Business Consultant* for this reason; you as a business owner are looking for someone who has a broad base of business exposure. This exposure gives background, experience, perspective and most of all expertise to avoid common pitfalls. *The Primary Business Consultant* has this background.

Planning

Once a completed assessment is done then it is time to have a planning meeting. This can be done over a period of time or at a one-time meeting. The latter is our recommendation. This is a great time to go over the report and go through the recommendations and prepare the company and leadership for implementation of the Enhancement plan. We need to clarify that the issues most assessments discover are obvious. The business owner knows there are weaknesses and struggles now. The key to Enhancement however is the implementation of the plan. That is the key component of this meeting. There has to be a commitment to implementation and follow through. If there is not, then our advice and recommendation is don't start.

Implementation

This is where the change takes place. This is where you begin to see the benefit of time and effort addressing these issues. There is a concept called the Hawthorne Effect. This concept simply states that any particular item that you choose to give attention automatically shows a 15% increase or reduction depending on what you are after when it is given attention. So we know that there is the base opportunity to see some benefit, however, it is the long term and equity building activity we seek.

We begin implementing by chasing the closest profit dollars possible. These opportunities are usually obvious, however, they have not been implemented. We have found that having an outside influence who can build the relationship and rapport with the people who are going to be involved in the change can be much more effective than trying to put an inside individual in charge of implementing these issues, many which are long standing or had failed attempts in the past.

Coaching is the best way to develop behavior that is continued past the point of initial discussion. Things such as better record systems and the reduction of unnecessary expenses, potential profit drains, and the cash flow strains of cyclical income can be addressed before they occur. If necessary, crisis management might include unpopular cost cutting, elimination of non-profitable products and services and a determined effort at timely collection of accounts receivable.

Coaching also involves helping you balance all budgets, which should be one of your first commitments. This means spend less than you make from day one and never violate the principle. Inventory management, cash flow management and other cost cuting designs will be part of your game plan.

Aggressive strategies will be decided upon and part of the implementation will be improving services, products, public image, customer relations, and employee relations. All of these improve bottom line profits and ultimate business value. Problems avoided are much less expensive than problems solved.

Financing and proper balance of funding is important to Enhancing business ownership! Proper funding and cash flow management are the ingredients that make it possible for many businesses to prosper. We believe the greatest stress in business centers around the cash flow issue. Countless companies caught in this bootstrapping syndrome have lost their equity because they have not solved the cash flow issue. Improper funding causes many wonderful ideas to never reach their potential or possibly fail. The proper balance of debt and equity is your goal! There is the other side. Too much debt is just as dangerous as insufficient funding. Some get drunk with capital not realizing what the burn rate is and end up with poor cash flow. This can also tempt you to temporarily become over confident and relax the disciplined actions necessary to stay on a profitable course. The ultimate loss would be to owe more to someone else, losing control and bottom line profits from your own ideas and efforts.

Several important factors determine how much you should borrow. You must be sure you have the personal commitment to assume the additional responsibility. Remember, your net cash flow must be increased to compensate for the additional debt service. Additional funding increases the possibility of losing personal equity. Additional collateral must be provided to most lenders and investors. It is important that the reasons and expectations of gains from borrowing exceed the risks.

You must choose the proper types(s) of debt and keep them balanced with your needs and ability to repay. You should use good planning between interim, short-term and long-term borrowing. Other considerations might include factoring (or less factoring) of accounts receivable, line(s) of credit, letter(s) of credit, asset guaranteed loans, personally guaranteed loans, inventory loans, bonded loans, equipment financing, credit card borrowing, floor planning, and several other types. With proper planning and careful screening there will be adequate resources available to you!

The major shortcoming of the "old style business broker" is the fact that they never sold the majority of the businesses they took to the market. A recent survey among some of the more successful ones indicated that over 50% of the businesses they took to the market never sold and that many of them should never have been taken to the market! In fact one indicated that 90% of the businesses on which he had taken marketing assignments were not adequately prepared.

Why did these unfortunate businesses never sell at their highest potential value? The reason is plain and simple. First, the owners did not secure an adequate third-party appraisal to determine an accurate value. Second, when the current value did not indicate the highest potential value desired, they did not secure an additional Business Enhancement Report from a *Primary Business Consultant* to learn what they needed to do to accomplish the higher value. Consequently, many of the businesses were sold at prices much less than what was desired and could have ultimately been accomplished.

An independent third-party business appraisal that reveals a value less than desired is not necessarily bad news. It can be a blessing in disguise. When your physician indicates the receipt of a preliminary test with a less than desired result, often there are remedies that can produce an even better ultimate outcome. Such is the case with your business appraisal. If you will take proper actions, current profits and ultimate value can be dramatically increased. A properly trained *Primary Business Consultant* can secure an additional independent third-patty Business Enhancement Report that will indicate what can be accomplished to give you increased current earnings and ultimate value.

Why should an Entering business owner consider an Enhancement Business Plan? Lending institutions will look more favorably at aggressive financing if you present them with a Business Enhancement Plan that justifies the financing. The first thing you should do upon Entering business ownership is to implement a Business Enhancement Plan. This will increase your productions and profits from the beginning and ultimately produce a higher business value.

You should take advantage of the benefits of a Business Enhancement Plan in every phase of your business ownership cycle!

Primary Business Consultants are available "on demand" to help you with problem solving at any time. More importantly, they can be of more value to you when allowed to assist in problem prevention through a Business Enhancement plan.

BUSINESS OWNERSHIP CYCLE

PRIMARY BUSINESS CONSULTANTS
Coach The Entrepreneur Through All Phases!

EXITING BUSINESS OWNERSHIP

*One can live magnificently in this world if one
knows how to work and how to love, to work for
the person one loves and to love one's work.*
Leo Tolstoy

At some point, the owner of every business will consider an Exit strategy to cash in on years of hard work and investment. If you have a current interest in Exiting your business, or considering maximizing the value of your business for a future Exit, this is an excellent time to make your move.

Some financial experts think we are at, or near, the top of an unparalleled growth cycle for independently owned businesses in America. Businesses are selling for the highest prices in history! Realistically, no one can predict how long this will last.

It is never too soon to start planning your Exit strategy. Such major decisions require careful planning and educated decisions. In chapter one we explained the benefits of using *Primary Business Consultants* and now is the time for you to contact one.

Your business is probably your most valuable asset and your Exit from it should be treated as one of the most important things you will ever accomplish. In over three decades of serving clients in their Exit strategy, we have observed that successful transactions all contain common ingredients.

First, there must be a strong desire and commitment that an ownership transfer actually takes place. Some businesses are just not salable. However, some good businesses never sell for reasons other than those caused by negative aspects of the business. Many do not sell because those responsible fail to make proper and timely decisions regarding steps necessary to consummate a sale, merger or family transition. Consequently, your first concern is to select a *Primary Business Consultant* to guide the process through each important phase.

The <u>second, and possibly most important ingredient</u> is to assure that the business goes to market at the highest achievable price. Be sure you read chapter two to better understand the importance of an appraisal of your business. Surely, no one should ever consider Exiting their most important asset without first securing a professional business appraisal from an independent third-party who values businesses on a national basis. Your *Primary Business Consultant* will coordinate the flow of information to assure the most accurate appraisal of your company.

Even though the financial institution providing the purchase funds for the Entering client will require one anyway, it is imperative that you secure an appraisal of your own first to be sure you are not leaving money on the table. It would be tragic to find out after you've already agreed to a amount, that you accepted a lesser price than you could have achieved with the use of your own appraisal. You will be at a disadvantage if you allow the Entering party to be the only party with an appraisal. He/she may have succeeded in driving the price down by providing incomplete information to the appraiser. Your *Primary Business Consultant* knows how to dress up your business in its best "tuxedo and bow tie" and provide information to the appraiser that will allow you to support the price to your advantage.

Many of the better prospects for your business may come from other states and in some instances other countries. We live in an era of globalization and all of us are affected by what happens elsewhere. It would be a mistake to ignore trends in other economic markets, especially if to use them would be to your benefit. Use an appraiser with national/international experience in order to take advantage of higher pricing patterns supported in areas with better economies. An independent third-party appraiser with significant experience in all types of businesses and ample comparable data to support his/her decisions will have credibility to impress the Entering prospect and his/her advisors.

Anytime you are involved in a business transaction, you would be wise to at least consider the possibility that your decisions and actions may be later challenged in a court of law. Therefore, choose an appraiser who could best support you in such an extreme occurrence.

Avoiding the use of compromising professionals is the third ingredient in a successful transfer or Exit. *Primary Business Consultants* will serve as your advocate, working to achieve the highest rewards for the years of personal sacrifice you have invested in your business. Advocate is the strongest word we could find to express the need for a professional who will place your interest above every other interest in the transaction. A careful reading of chapter one will give you a good understanding of the type of relationship you need with the professional(s) guiding you through your Exit plan.

If the appraiser's opinion of value does not meet your requirements, ask your *Primary Business Consultant* to explain the advantages of an Enhancement Plan. Chapter four provides the details of this strategy, which can significantly increase the value of your business.

If the appraisal you have received reflects an appropriate price to meet your needs, then it's time for you to investigate the most successful method of Exiting business ownership, which is known as the **Targeted Marketing Plan,** provided exclusively by *Primary Business Consultants*. You should have a "comfort zone" with your *Primary Business Consultant's* dedication to representing your interests above all others. Some states require that this relationship be defined in writing.

You also need a fair fee structure for the services you will receive from the *Primary Business Consultant* and other professionals you use. Expenses in the marketing process generally fall into six categories. The (1) incidental fees will be the same with the use of a professional as they would be if you were selling the business yourself. Because they deal in much larger volumes, your *Primary Business Consultant* can secure many of these services cheaper than they are available to you. You can control these costs using an agreement that initially spells out the maximum amount to be spent in your behalf each month. These costs should be billed to you on a monthly basis and will often be deducted from the final success fee you will owe at the consummation of the transaction.

Even though they may work many hours in your interest each month, your *Primary Business Consultant* will often only charge you a small (2) *monthly administrative fee* based only on a minimum number of hours. This fee will also often be deducted from the final success fee. This serves as the "no fault" insurance policy for your representative to keep him/her working with maximum effort, even though they are aware that you may not accept the offers they bring to you.

There should also be a (3) *minimum total fee* guaranteed to the *Primary Business Consultant* in the event you decide to sell to someone like a relative for as little as $1.00. Should you need your *Primary Business Consultant* to provide other services for which other professionals would normally be paid, you will be charged the going rate for (4) *other services*, such as real estate services, loan brokerage, "head hunter" fees, etc.

The (5) *final success fee* will be due to your *Primary Business Consultant* at the consummation of the transaction. As previously stated, the monthly administrative and incidental fees will often be deducted from this final fee at the closing table.

Fees for services from (6) *other professionals* such as attorneys, accountants, etc., will be paid at the conclusion of these services, or on such terms as these professionals are engaged.

The average time taken to consummate a transaction is nine months. However, because of the difficulties of marketing some businesses, the length of time involved in your commitment to the *Primary Business Consultant* should be a minimum of twelve months.

The Exiting business owner should be involved in the Targeted Marketing Plan. In fact, immediately upon signing an agreement with a *Primary Business Consultant*, you will be asked for a minimum participation in preparing the information to be shared with Entering prospects.

You should receive written monthly reports of all activities as well as a preview of activities for the next month for your approval. Your participation and approval in the planning, execution and budgeting of your Exiting plan is very important. You want to be sure something is accomplished on a regular basis and that your expenditures are spent exclusively on your business. The Targeted Marketing Plan used by your *Primary Business Consultant* can include over fifty different options, all of which are "targeted" to specific prospects who are more likely to be interested in your individual business. Don't allow your business to be involved in the old style general marketing process where it could be placed in a large pool of businesses with little or no individual attention and possibly over exposed to people who have no interest in your industry.

The exclusive Targeted Marketing Plan provided by your *Primary Business Consultant* is a " win-win" for all involved in your Exit strategy. First, it is a "win" for you the Exiting owner in the following ways:

1. You receive a fair expenditure of funds because there are no "free-loaders." Your money is spent specifically in the marketing of your *own* business, instead of being spent on a lot of businesses in a general marketing pool of businesses.

2. You enjoy the superior advantage and peace of mind of un-compromised advocacy from your *Primary Business Consultant*. Since you are participating in the expenses, your professional can afford to wait for the best offer instead of trying to talk you into a lesser offer, just so he/she can make a commission.

3. You are assured of the best, consistent efforts from your consultant because you must receive and approve monthly reports of activities. Your consultant works harder and faster because they don't want their final success fee to be eroded by unnecessary monthly fees. Because you are participating in the costs, the consultant can afford to do what is best for you, not just what is best for their pocket book. Your *Primary Business Consultant* has been trained in over 50 discrete activities to locate and attract appropriate Entering prospects, thereby increasing the likelihood of accomplishing your transaction.

4. You retain the timely veto power on any activities because you must approve everything a month in advance of its use.

5. Your personal involvement in these decisions gives you control over the final outcome.

6. Your financial participation makes your serious motivations more believable to Entering prospects. This will motivate them to bring their best offer(s) sooner.

7. You receive a much higher quality of service that costs you no more, because your monthly financial participation is credited to the success fee you owe at the end. Your *Primary Business Consultant* can tell you up front what your total costs will be and place a "cap" on them at that total amount.

8. Targeted marketing to more legitimate prospects assures a more confidential process.

9. The targeted marketing process creates conditions for better participation by other professionals involved in your transaction:

a. Attorneys, bankers, accountants and other advisors are more likely to participate positively and with less apprehension because you have not used a compromising consultant.

b. Normal steps involved in due-diligence and financing will move much faster because information presented is more professional and believable.

c. The closing process will be less expensive because proper steps have been taken in the collection and preparation of all relevant information.

d. Other members of your advisory "team" will respect you more because of the professionalism of your *Primary Business Consultant* who operates on a level to which they are accustomed to working.

You need to have full confidence that anyone engaged for such a vital role is properly motivated and compensated to do their best for you at all times. Your *Primary Business Consultant* is no exception. In the Targeted Marketing Plan it ultimately costs you no more to get the best service. Since your monthly financial participation makes it possible for them to do what is best for you, and, you get credit for these costs against the final success fee, it is a win-win for all parties. This assures you of their best efforts, and here's why:

1. They are assured of your genuine commitment.

2. They are provided funds for incidental expenses, which you approve, and which assures you of un-compromising decisions.

3. Because of the required monthly reports, they now have specific milestones to accomplish with a definite working plan on which they can put maximum effort and achieve quicker success.

4. They now have adequate cash flow to do what they know is best for you.

5. The proper, effective use of funds is important to them because they know each expenditure is taken out of their final

success fee.

6. They work harder and faster because they realize they are ultimately spending their own money.

7. These *Primary Business Consultant*s will earn more fees over a career because of better consistent efforts on more quality assignments.

If you do not enter into a win-win arrangement with the professional(s) working for you, much less will be accomplished, and here's why:

1. They cannot afford to do much because no quality professional can personally afford to pay for what's best for <u>every</u> client.

2. They are not committed to do much because they cannot commit to what they cannot afford.

3. The client cannot expect much because they are not financially committed.

4. There are no specific milestones connected to a step-by-step plan.

Now you know why you don't want to commit your business to the old style general marketing used by some "brokers" in the marketplace. There won't be much success because there is no real commitment connected to specific milestones and because there are not proper funds available. You can make a full commitment to a *Primary Business Consultant* because they will give you their best effort. They do this because funds are available and you will be expecting regular reports or you will cut off the funds!

The <u>fourth ingredient</u> of a successful Exit strategy is the concern for confidentiality. In chapter three we discussed how you could maintain confidentiality in the entire process. Please review this for a review of these important considerations.

Choosing the other professionals you need and knowing when to use them is the <u>fifth ingredient</u> you must allow your

Primary Business Consultant to monitor for you. In chapter one we shared with you the advantages of allowing a *Primary Business Consultant* to be the "coach" of the entire team that guides you through all stages of business ownership, especially the Exit plan.

Timing is an important aspect of any important event. The *Primary Business Consultant* is your clock-watcher to be sure that every professional you use performs in a timely manner. They have dealt with most concerns many times and their professional checklists will help everyone perform at their best. Some of these check lists are:

1. Proper presentation of vital information regarding your business, which is presented to legitimate Entering prospects.

2. A list of over fifty activities for use in locating the best match in an Entering prospect for your business.

3. Items of importance to you that should be included in an offer to purchase presented to you.

4. An analysis of offers presented to you.

5. Items of importance included in Counteroffer(s) you make.

6. Important concerns in the removal of contingencies from offers.

7. Concerns for extension of offers presented to you.

8. Vital information used in closing documents.

9. Concerns for your protection at the closing table.

It is always fun to be a part of a winning team! You can be confident that the stress and negative aspects of professional egos will be kept to a minimum. The Exiting of your business is the crowning event of your business ownership career and is to be enjoyed. Your team will play hard for you; right up to the end...your coach (*Primary Business Consultant*) will see to it.

TYPES OF BUSINESS OWNERSHIP

Luck is where preparation meets opportunity.
Author Unknown

There are a number of different legal entities under which a business can be owned and operated. We will set forth some of them and some of the advantages and disadvantages of each method of ownership. Since the state codes regarding the forms of legal entities, corporations, partnerships, and limited liability companies are being constantly updated, you should check your own state laws if you have any questions about those codes.

Sole Proprietorship

The most common form of business ownership for small businesses is a sole proprietorship. It is a business in which all equity lies with one individual. For those states that operate under community property laws, both husband and wife own the business, even though the business license and title may be in only one of their names. If the business owner can clearly establish that the funds to purchase the business came from sources outside of those earned by the "community" (the married couple), then the business is the sole and separate property of that individual whose funds were used to start or purchase the business. With the sole proprietorship type of business ownership, the income of the business becomes the income of the owner and is reported as a part of the owner's personal income and reported on Schedule C of the tax return and is taxable directly to the owner.

When a sole proprietorship is operated under a name other than the owner's name, it is usually necessary to file in the county where the business is located and to obtain a "fictitious name" certificate enabling you to "do business as" under a name other than your own. This is commonly referred to as "d.b.a." This registers the name you wish to use and identifies the business owner as the person operating that business under a "fictitious name." Without having the certificate, most banks will not let you use the business name on your bank account and on your checks. If you ever find it necessary to file suit against a customer for failure to pay a bill with your fictitious name included as the creditor, you will need to produce a current certificate in order for the obligation to be recognized by the court.

One advantage in establishing your business as a sole proprietorship is that it puts you directly in control. There is no board of directors or partners to consult with before making a business decision. It also has the advantage that it is probably the easiest type of business ownership for keeping accounting and bookkeeping records. There are no shareholders meetings or corporate minutes to keep.

When it comes time to Exit your sole proprietorship, another advantage is that the payment for the business goes directly to the owner. In comparison, in the case of a corporation, unless an Entering prospect is buying the stock in your corporation, it is the corporation, which is selling its corporate assets to the buyer, and as a result the funds for the sale go directly to the corporation. For the shareholder in turn to receive any money from the transaction, the individual shareholder must find a method for withdrawing the proceeds from the corporation for the sale of those assets. The main disadvantage of a sole proprietorship is that, in the event of a lawsuit, the proprietor would be personally liable and all of his assets, including the "non-business" assets would be at risk in the event of losing the lawsuit.

Partnerships
Many times friends or family members decide to go into

business together as partners. A partnership is a contractual relationship between two or more people in a joint enterprise, who agree to share, not necessarily equally in the profits and losses of the organization. Note the word "contractual" in that definition. Many times partnerships are entered into without a written contract and with just a "hand shake." Sometimes good friends believe that the trust between them is all that is necessary. However, it is always prudent to have a carefully drawn contractual agreement setting forth all of the terms of the partnership.

In setting up a partnership, it is important to designate such items as (a) capital contributions, (b) allocation of income and expense, and (c) the methods of decision-making.

Partnerships **always** end. It could be divorce or death of one partner, etc., but it will end. Likewise, a business partnership will end and it is critical in the agreement that the ending is clearly delineated. The fair market value at the time the partnership ends is a most important consideration of the terms in the agreement in order to insure a litigation free termination. Although contracts are written and agreed to in good faith, carrying out those terms is not always fair or easy. To set the business value at the time the partnership agreement is first written could produce legal headaches years later. Price and terms determined at the beginning of the partnership would not take into consideration the change in value during the term of that partnership. The best method is for the parties to agree to engage the services of a qualified business appraiser on an annual basis, as well as at the time of the termination of the partnership, to determine the fair market value. If the partners cannot decide on using such services, and they resort to legal action, they will learn that the court will probably hire an appraiser and the judge will decide what the business is worth.

When individuals decide to form a partnership, as indicated above, they should determine very carefully who will do what and how the income will be allocated, but rarely is enough thought given to how they will end the partnership on a fair and equitable basis. Will the departing partner be able to sell her/his share to an outsider? Will the remaining partner(s) have the first option and at what price formula and terms? Will they buy life insurance to fund a buy out in the event of the death of a partner?

If you insist on entering into a partnership, make absolutely certain that all of the terms and conditions of that partnership are clearly set forth in the agreement. Even the best of friends or family members will disagree, but the method of resolving any such disagreements needs to be clearly understood. Otherwise a court may have to make the decision for you.

Our opinion is that you can avoid many of the problems inherent in having partners and that the most satisfactory way to operate any business is with control of that business. If you are truly an entrepreneur, you can always find qualified and dependable people to work with you. However, for any company to be successful someone needs to be responsible for the profitable operation of that business, and that person is the woman or man at the top, who is in charge. As in the case of a sole proprietorship, the downside of a partnership is that there is potential for being personally liable for each of the partners. This risk exists for any partner, not only for his/her own acts and omissions, but also for those acts and omissions committed by others.

Limited Partnership

A recent development in entity law is a creation of a Limited Liability Partnership, which over-lays a "corporate veil" of protection over the traditional partnership structure. A limited partnership is an entity wherein the limited partners of the partnership are not personally liable for debts and liabilities of the partnership. However, by law, at least one partner must be fully liable and that partner becomes the General Partner. Usually under the partnership agreement, the General Partner usually conducts the affairs of the partnership as it sees fit. In the event of a loss, a limited partner can only lose the original invested amount, plus any subsequent investments made in the partnership. Thus the "limited partners" are limited.

There are also Professional Corporations and Limited Liability Partnerships. These are usually made up of members of specific professions such as accountants or attorneys. When professionals form such a professional business relationship, they often form a Limited Liability Partnership or an "L.L.P." where a partner is not liable for a negligent act committed by another partner or by an employee not under the partner's supervision.

Corporation

A corporation is an entity (usually a business) having authority under law to act as a single person distinct from the shareholders who own it and having rights to issue stock and exist indefinitely.

Please note one important feature of a corporation, which is different from a proprietorship, is that it can "exist indefinitely." Others can acquire the shares of stock and the corporation can continue past your lifetime and past subsequent owners' lifetimes.

Most beginning entrepreneurs become interested in forming corporations rather than operating as a sole proprietorship because in most instances the corporation is solely responsible for any liabilities it incurs in doing business. Some shareholders find that being shielded personally from possible losses and liabilities is an appealing idea. Such protection from personal liability requires complete confirmation to your state's corporation laws in terms of Shareholder Meetings and Board of Director Meetings for which detailed minutes must be kept. It is essential that the corporation act in the manner required by law in order to maintain the "corporate veil" which protects the shareholder(s) from creditors.

From a practical standpoint, most small corporations when seeking credit or signing for space leases or for equipment leases are asked by the leasing or credit grantors for personal guarantees by the principal shareholder, who is usually the CEO or President of the corporation. For a shareholder to refuse to personally guarantee such a request tells the credit grantor that the owner does not have enough faith in the success of the corporation to meet its obligations and that can be the reason for denial of the credit request. Since the owner of most corporations wants and needs the credit they are requesting, they will sign personally. Usually they have the confidence that the corporation will be able meet its obligations, and so they are willing to sign personally. When personal guarantees are given, the protection from the "corporate shield" no longer exists. If the corporation is unable to pay, the personal guarantor becomes liable.

If and when it becomes necessary for a creditor to take legal action against the corporation where that creditor has no personal guarantee, the creditor's attorney seeks whatever means are necessary to "pierce the corporate veil" so they can go directly to the individual for collection of the obligation. Unless the corporate minutes and all the legal requirements of the operating the corporation are kept accurately on a regular basis, it is likely that the creditor's legal experts will find a way to pursue the individual personally.

The disadvantages described above for a corporation in comparison with a sole proprietorship or partnership, do not outweigh the advantages for the business where substantial growth is projected and where it is possible that the initial shareholder(s) may want to sell or give as an incentive bonus some shares of stock in the corporation. Using a corporation to own and operate one's business clearly separates the shareholder's personal activities and their business activities.

From a taxation viewpoint, there are two types of corporations that we would like to describe at this time. Both corporations embody the original corporation concept which was defined above as "an entity which is legally able to operate as a person distinct from it owners." This form of corporation is commonly referred to as a "C" corporation. The term "C Corp" came into usage to differentiate one corporation from the other type which operates under Subchapter S of the Internal Revenue Code, and hence is commonly called an "S Corp."

An "S Corp" is a corporation in fact, but it is taxed as a partnership. All of the profits of the "S Corp" become taxable to the individual shareholder(s) in direct ratio to their stock ownership. The taxes are payable on those earnings regardless of whether the funds have been distributed to the shareholder(s) or not. It should be noted that if the "S Corp" has a loss, that loss becomes a personal tax deduction for the shareholder(s) in direct proportion to their holdings.

Normally, "S Corp" shareholders who are employees of the corporation earn salaries just as they do in a "C Corp" and are subject to the same personal tax liability for those earnings. How operating a "C Corp" would differ from operating as an "S Corp" is a subject for the entrepreneur to discuss with competent tax and legal consultants. The advantages and disadvantages of each type should be clearly understood before selecting the one appropriate for you.

At the time a business goes on the market to be sold, the owner, shareholders, or partners should discuss the sale and the tax consequences of the sale with their *Primary Business Consultant* and a qualified tax consultant in order to understand their tax liability. It is of utmost importance that you know what, if any taxes, you might anticipate upon the completion of the transaction.

There are several other designations given to a corporation, which we would like to identify at this time. It should be remembered however, that these designations merely clarify the general nature and purpose of the corporation, but they are still a "C Corp" or an "S Corp" at all times. A Close Corporation or Closed Corporation or Closely Held Corporation is one whose stock is not freely traded and is held by only a few shareholders, usually officers, employees, or others close to the management. The requirements and privileges of close corporations vary by state and your attorney can explain what they are for your state.

Collapsible Corporation is one formed to give a short-term venture the appearance of a long-term investment, which is terminated when the short-term objective has been reached.

Limited Liability Companies
Limited-Liability Company also termed Limited-Liability Corporation is a company statutorily authorized in a certain state, which is characterized by limited liability, management by members or managers, and has limitation on ownership transfer. It is known as an "L.L.C."

Joint Venture
Another type of business called a Joint Venture is a commercial undertaking by two or more people or entities, differing from a partnership by relating to the disposition of a single lot of goods or the termination of a specific project.

Terminology
At this point there are several other terms in the business vocabulary, which we would like to discuss. One is a Merger, which results from the combining of two or more entities

through the direct acquisition by one entity of the net assets of the other(s). A merger differs from a consolidation in that the merger creates no new entity, whereas in a consolidation a new organization comes into being and acquires the assets of all the combining units.

A second term used frequently is Lease and it is a form of contract transferring the use or occupancy of land, space structures, or equipment, in consideration of a payment, usually in the form of rent. In a lease, the lessor gives the use of the property to a lessee.

Another one is a Tax Free (deferred) "1031" Exchange which constitutes the transfer of property that the tax laws specifically exempts from income tax consequences. Although real estate is frequently sold on a like-kind exchange, which defers the taxes until sometime in the future, the process, though legal, is not often used in the sale of business and requires a consultant thoroughly familiar with its use when considering the sale of your company on a tax-free exchange.

We would now like to describe briefly another way of exiting your company that was conceived as a method for employee participation in the ownership in the business where the employee works. Properly used, it can stimulate loyalty and create a true proprietary interest in the company's welfare on the part of each employee.

ESOP

It is called the Employee Stock Ownership Plan or "ESOP." While the Plan is complex in its many ramifications, essentially it enables a shareholder to sell for cash any or all of her/his shares to a Trust formed with the ESOP, and the proceeds of such sale are capital gains tax deferred when those funds are invested in US domestic securities (other than land or mutual funds). The capital gains tax deferment continues so long as the investments are held and the deferment can be passed on to the heirs of the shareholder.

The use of an ESOP is an ideal way to purchase an exiting shareholder's shares so that the Exiting shareholder gets fair market value for the shares, gets the cash, and so long as the proceeds are invested as required within 12 months of the receipt of the funds, the Exiting shareholder can defer the capital gains tax normally due.

The corporation wishing to inaugurate an ESOP must be a "C Corp" and have been under the same management for three years. An "S Corp" can be converted to a "C Corp" at the time of the installation of the ESOP in order to conform to the law.

The Trust, which is formed to own and to vote the shares on behalf of the employee participants in the ESOP, borrows the money from the corporation to fund the purchase of shares from the Exiting shareholder. The corporation borrows the money from a bank or other lender, and that lender loans the money to the corporation, who, in turn, loans it to the Trust, which pays the Exiting shareholder for the shares.

In order to qualify for the tax advantages the Trust must own or acquire at least 30% of the outstanding shares of the corporation. The method of repayment of the loan is itself a tax-deductible expense to the corporation. Each year the corporation can make a tax-deductible contribution to the Trust on behalf of the participating employees in an amount not to exceed 25% of the total payroll of those participants. In addition, the corporation can make additional tax-deductible contributions of reasonable dividends to the Trust. It is through these contributions to the Trust, which enable it to repay the loan.With an ESOP, a corporation and Exiting shareholder(s) can "have their cake and eat it too" so to speak. A deferred capital gains tax payment for shares of corporate stock is actually funded with tax-deductible dollars.

An independent third party appraisal of the corporation is

required to initiate the ESOP and is also required annually so that any exiting employee will receive the latest fair market price for their shares which the company buys back as stipulated in the original Plan agreement. Employees are given the right to accumulate corporate stock for their account in the ESOP without any financial contribution of their own. When they leave the employment of the corporation for any reason, other than for criminal charges, they are entitled to the value of their shares as determined by the most recent annual independent third-party appraisal.

An ESOP requires several very competent consultants. The first one is an independent consultant thoroughly familiar with ESOP's who can work with corporate management as to whether the Plan is suitable for the corporation. Also absolutely necessary is an attorney well versed in ESOP matters who represents the ESOP Trust. The corporation's attorney is always involved representing the company, so that there is no conflict of interest between the Trust and the company. In order to conform to the IRS requirements, the independent third party business appraiser is needed. That appraiser should have ESOP valuation experience and will perform the initial appraisal and subsequent annual required up dated appraisals. While the start up costs for an ESOP are not insignificant, the savings to both the selling shareholder(s) and the corporation are enormous.

While it is possible for an Exiting shareholder to sell some of hers/his shares to a new owner of the business and the balance to the ESOP Trust, many times the ESOP will purchase 100% of the shares. When this occurs, the participants elect a board of directors and that board names the officers who will manage the business.

Many Exiting business owners justifiably feel that the cooperation and the loyalty of the employees are what made that company successful. What better way to recognize that feeling towards the employees than by giving them shares in the business and getting paid in capital gains tax deferred cash at the same time? It is a win, win situation.

There is another and tremendously advantageous use of an ESOP. If expansion capital is needed for a growing corporation, additional treasury stock can be issued to the ESOP, which then pays the corporation for that stock enabling the corporation to generate working capital for growth. And again the loan by the company to fund the purchase is repaid with tax-deductible contributions to the Trust.

It should be clear in examining the various kinds of types of business ownership and the resulting considerations that arise during the Entering, operating and Exiting a business, that a successful entrepreneur should find and engage the services of a competent *Primary Business Consultant* who can be their primary contact and source whenever important business decisions need to be made. Such a consultant can guide the business owner to an attorney, an accountant, a business appraiser or any other needed expert when services are required.

FINANCING A TRANSFER OF
BUSINESS OWNERSHIP

The poor man is not he who is without a cent,
but he who is without a dream.
Harry Kemp

There is probably no area of greater consequence to the successful transfer of business ownership than the arrangement of proper financing. While the number of privately held businesses that are transferred on an all cash basis can not be known, experience shows that where an Exiting owner's financing is not an option, he/she can expect to receive offers with a discount factor of 10-20%.

To receive the maximum value, an owner should consider providing some financing. This could reflect an additional increase in value. In many cases, the Exiting party will allow the Entering party to pay a portion of the price as a down payment at closing and to pay the remaining balance over a scheduled time frame plus interest. This is beneficial to the owner because the owner can earn additional interest income for many years. In fact, a carry-back loan will significantly increase the total amount the Exiting owner receives. The Exiting owner should consider the favorable tax treatment resulting from the installment approach for with deferred payments the tax due from that portion is also deferred.

Many Exiting owners seek to maximize the net proceeds from a sale or transfer because of specific personal financial objectives. However, most Exiting owners who want "all cash" or want to collect as much as possible at the closing are attempting to protect themselves from the risk of a business take back or a failed transfer.

The Exiting owner may fear that the Entering entrepreneur might not operate the business as well. Such fears may be reasonable, given the evident inexperience of a particular Entering entrepreneur.

In contrast, most Entering entrepreneurs prefer to invest as little as possible at closing and spread their payments out as far as possible.

Usually, the Entering entrepreneur feels more comfortable if the Exiting owner continues to have a serious financial interest in the business so that any future problems can be dealt with through the Exiting owner, at least near term.

In many successful business transfers, an agreement is struck, involving an initial investment that is reasonable, but substantial enough to protect the Exiting owner's assets. Often, the minimum down amounts ranges from 25% to 40% of the purchase price.

Both Exiting and Entering parties have expenses at closing and one or the other has an agreed obligation to pay the *Primary Business Consultant*, at closing, for securing the other party.

A professional business appraisal produced, in advance, by an independent third-party will provide an improved comfort level for the parties involved in negotiating a business transfer. The Entering entrepreneur will know that the values are both real and justifiable. The Exiting owner is assured he/she is both asking and receiving a market price for both assets and business value.

In the case of an asset sale, generally the Exiting owner will keep the accounts receivables, cash in the bank, investment cash, paid up life insurance, and other "liquid" assets. Exiting owners who feel the need to protect themselves further have the option of requiring a larger down payment, or to require additional collateral from the Entering entrepreneur, which might include other assets such as equity in real estate. However, insistence that the Entering party pledge assets outside the business usually becomes a major negative, whether set out in the marketing package or raised later during negotiations.

An Exiting owner who agrees to partially finance a business transfer may decide that he/she does not want to receive payments and interest for the full term of the note. In that case they may have the option of selling the carry back note to any number of companies who purchase such "stream of payments", especially if there is a documented record of timely payments over a period of time.

This purchase of the note will provide all the cash to the Exiting owner at the time the note is purchased (less a fee) and the Entering entrepreneur will continue to make payments as prescribed in the original agreement. Alternatively, the purchase of "Buy Out Bonds" (insurance) that will guarantee the principal and interest payments may ease the Exiting Owner's fears about carrying back a portion of the purchase price.

Bank Financing Options

An Entering entrepreneur who has established a long-term, positive borrowing and repayment relationship with a banker will probably look favorably on a new business acquisition loan. This would be even more likely if the loan application were supported by an independent third-party business appraisal.

A second banking option would be to have the Exiting owner introduce the Entering entrepreneur to his/her long-term banker. Given that banker's extensive knowledge of the existing business he/she would, in most instances, feel more comfortable with the business loan to a qualified Entering candidate. Most bankers would want to continue a good relationship with an existing business.

New banks that are trying to establish themselves in the community may represent another source of funding. These new banks are sometimes more aggressive than their more established competitors and might consider loans that aren't granted by larger competitors. Depending on bank management, particular banks may or may not be granting acquisition loans at a given time. Typically internal policies, goals, and quotas guide these decisions.

Government Guaranteed Loans

Federal, state or local government agencies offer loans or loan guarantees in situations where there is a public policy interest, such as when it can be shown that a successful loan will benefit the local economy or improve employment possibilities in a particular community or area. Included among these are:

1. Small Business Administration
(Many types are available)
2. United States Department of Agriculture
Guaranteed Loans
(Usually approved to assist undeveloped areas)
3. State Industrial Revenue Bonds

Small Business Administrations Loans (SBA)

These loans are for businesses that employ less than 500 employees. They can be made for as much as 90% of the purchase price. Very few of these loans are made directly by the Small Business Administration. Very small special opportunity loans ($25,000 to $100,00) are government granted. However, banks throughout the United States who participate in SBA lending programs grant most SBA loans. These banks take the applications, process them, and submit for federal government approval.

When the loan is approved for SBA guarantee participation, the bank grants the loan and directly disburses the proceeds to the borrower. The loan is then serviced by the participating bank throughout the life of the loan. The Federal government does not provide any cash. It only serves in its role as guarantor. If the loan goes into default, the government authorizes its percentage guarantee and pays the bank that portion. In most cases the guarantee ranges from 75% to 90%. This percentage depends on the type of business involved and the details of the transaction. The best place to start is with your local banker who is already familiar with you and your credit.

Alternatively, one might start with a Preferred SBA Lender. These lenders are very experienced with the SBA loan process and have previously shown good underwriting procedures to the SBA. The preferred lender designation means they have been given the authority to grant SBA loans without SBA advance approval. This really speeds up the process. As we all know, most government-originated programs require a tremendous amount of paperwork. Without an experienced person handling the SBA process, it can become very lengthy and tedious.

Some banks have specialized departments who process SBA loans because of their complexity. Since banks are ultimately responsible for only 10% to 25% of the total loan, they are sometimes willing to take a larger level of risk than normal. This type of loan can sometimes be helpful for banks that are concerned about their CRA ratings with the FDIC and/or Federal Reserve. CRA is a government abbreviation for Community Redevelopment Act. Each bank is scored on a variety of items, including serving their lower-income neighborhoods and the disadvantaged. Some FDIC and Federal Reserve audits include maps showing specific communities where loans have been granted and the racial make-up of those areas. An unacceptable CRA rating can serve as the basis for denying existing banks authorization to open new offices or withhold approval from a proposed bank merger until they improve.

The SBA also has what it refers to as a No-Doc loan, i.e. No Documentation loans which purposely require no documentation or at least in the government purview, no documentation. The maximum amount granted on a No-Doc SBA loan is $100,000.

The Federal government also authorizes **non-bank** lenders to grant SBA loans. These non-bank entities qualify their loans in much the same manner as banks. A number of these non-bank lenders are specialists in these loans and can complete the qualification and underwriting process faster than most banks.

1. Some non-bank lenders will review the relevant financial documents and offer a **tentative** advance approval for financing a transfer prior to a business being sold.

2. Such pre-qualification is always subject to approval of a qualified Entering entrepreneur.

3. In all of these loans the borrowers credit, character and collateral are of the utmost importance.

4. Business collateral is less important for some non-bank lenders who are willing to consider a business with good cash flow but with few or no assets.

5. Other requirements include provable income and expenses, no outstanding tax liens, and future projections of income.

A second type of government loan is guaranteed by what may seem like an unlikely source, the United States Department of Agriculture. In order to assist economically under-developed counties throughout the United States, loan guarantees can be up to $10,000,000 and terms up to 25 years can be obtained. Such uses include acquisition and expansion of commercial businesses, housing projects, nursing and rest home facilities, and local water and sewer projects. Contact can be made through a local USDA office or use the USDA website to get information about the nearest office.

Obstacles An Entering Entrepreneur May Encounter Acquiring Financing

In the process of securing financing for Entering a business, there are a number of dangers that may be encountered. One is the lack of complete financial information provided by the Exiting owner of the business. The financial history of the business may not be consistently presented to allow the Entering entrepreneur to feel comfortable with the information. In the interest of both parties; it is beneficial to have an independent third-party business appraisal prepared. The gathering, formatting and analyzing of financial information require the services of a trained person who is experienced in appraising businesses. The costs associated with a major mistake in valuing and pricing of a business can be disastrous. The expense of an independent third-party appraisal would be relatively small in comparison. A *Primary Business Consultant* will not advise that a business ownership transfer take place without an independent third-party business appraisal. Any professional who would not recommend that an independent third-party appraisal be produced, would make someone question his or her un-compromised objectivity.

Often the misuse of industry "Rules Of Thumb," earnings multiples and other ratios can cause an entrepreneur to either undervalue or overvalue a business. These "numbers" can be skewed very badly when differences in business accounting procedures are overlooked. It is critical for the entrepreneur to require an independent third-party appraisal to determine true market value.

Another obstacle in obtaining financing could be the lender's need to evaluate the Entering entrepreneurs' business plan. Lenders usually require projected future sales and income, clear indication of how the loan can be paid off using the business cash flow and the time needed for this payoff to occur. Conservative assumptions and projections are essential.

Another obstacle to securing proper financing might come from reliance on information and advice given by an inexperienced and/or compromised transaction attorney, accountant and/or other consultants.

Value of Professional Assistance

There are a variety of professionals in the business transfer industry. Some are, as is the case in any industry, more able to assist in specific areas than others. Here are some categories you may consider using to make the financing of a business ownership transfer easier, quicker, safer, and more fulfilling. Beware that some offer only "minimum services."

A. **Real Estate Brokers** usually trained in the selling of real estate only. Some of them will "list" your business for sale or show you what they have for sale. In most cases, they cannot help you Exit or Enter a particular business because there is not a successful national, (or local) multiple listing service established for businesses as there is for real estate for sale. Most real estate brokers are trained for offering residential real estate only (not ongoing businesses). There is usually no training available for them in financing business ownership transfers.

B. **Business Brokers** are specifically oriented brokers who have chosen to represent (in most cases) Exiting business owners. Many have only completed courses to educate them in how to "list" businesses for sale. Quite a number of these brokers represent too many businesses at one time. Some business brokers were previously involved only as real estate brokers and have no training in financing business transactions.

C. *Primary Business Consultants* are un-compromised professionals who are trained to assist those Entering or Exiting businesses in a variety of specific areas. The range includes identifying non-advertised businesses that may be available on the "hidden" market, confidentially handling transfers of businesses and offering guidance as to financing, structure, value and other un-compromised professionals who can be of assistance. One of their primary functions is to coordinate the activities of all the other professionals included in the endeavor. *Primary Business Consultant*s are familiar with a multitude of possibilities for financing businesses. *Primary Business Consultant*s recognize the importance of an independent third-party appraisal prior to the transfer of any business. Planning is also another area where *Primary Business Consultant*s provide guidance. They can provide projected income and expense forecasts for future use and also help identify and correct current problem areas in a business. They coordinate all aspects of the business transfer. *Primary Business Consultant*s can be particularly helpful in co-coordinating the work of the attorney, accountant, and lender in the transfer. The *Primary Business Consultant* in essence, serves as the coach of the overall transaction, as well as the financing.

TAX ASPECTS OF EXITING OWNERSHIP OF AN INDEPENDENTLY OWNED BUSINESS

*Be careful to stand up to your
responsibilities as vigorously
as you stand up for your rights.
Author Unknown*

There must be a clear sense of priorities in Exiting business ownership and the tax aspects are very important considerations. The first issue is to be sure you have chosen the appropriate un-compromised professional advocate (such as a *Primary Business Consultant*) to guide you through the entire process and to help you maintain control of each step.

Next, your *Primary Business Consultant* should monitor the securing of an independent third-party appraisal to protect the value you have achieved in your business. If the appraisal does not validate the price you need, he/she can then guide you through an Enhancement of the value of your business before your business is taken to the market.

Locating and negotiating with appropriate prospects to Enter ownership of your business is another area in which your *Primary Business Consultant* can provide the ultimate in client advocacy for you! His/her maximum marketing efforts will attract the best offers.

When you are ready to accept a legitimate offer you should have your *Primary Business Consultant* investigate the tax aspects with an independent third-party tax consultant. Together, they can provide appropriate tax strategies.

The tax aspects of Exiting your business can be rather

complex and depend on a variety of factors that could have a number of tax ramifications. We cannot make you aware of all the different tax issues of Exiting your business in this short discussion; however, we will help you consider the significant tax implications that can arise from what could be the most important business decision of your career.

Please understand that tax consequences can change and these statements are printed in keeping with tax laws as of this writing. This is why your *Primary Business Consultant* must guide you to the best tax specialists who understand the latest changes at the time of your transaction.

The first major factor in determining the tax effects of Exiting your business is the type of entity under which your business operates. There are different tax scenarios that depend on whether you are a proprietor, partnership, limited-liability company or corporation.

Proprietorships, Partnerships and Limited Liability Companies

If you are a proprietor, partnership or limited-liability company, the IRS currently states that the Exit of your business is not just the sale of one asset, but it is the sale of several assets. In general, when you Exit your business, each asset of your business is treated as if it were sold separately for the computation of gain or loss.

Both the Exiting and Entering parties involved in the ownership transfer of a business must report to the IRS the allocation of the sales price among the business assets involved in the transaction. This information is reported on Form 8594, *Asset Acquisition Statement Under Section 1060*. Both the Exiting and Entering parties need to attach Form 8594 to their federal income tax returns for the tax year in which the transaction occurred.

How to figure a gain or loss is illustrated in
the following table:

If:	Then:
Your adjusted basis in the assets sold is more than the amount you realized from the sale	You have a loss
The amount you realized from the sale is more than your adjusted basis in the assets sold	You have a gain

In order to determine if you have a gain or a loss, it is nec-essary to understand the following definitions:

Basis. The cost or purchase price of the property is usual-ly the basis of the property. However, if you acquired the prop-erty by gift, inheritance or in some other way than buying it, then other rules apply. You should consult with your tax advi-sor in these cases.

Adjusted basis. The adjusted basis of the property is your original basis plus certain additions, such as improvements, and minus certain deductions such as depreciation and casu-alty losses.

Amount realized. The amount realized from a sale is all the money you receive plus the fair market value of any prop-erty or services that you may receive as part of the sale. In addition, the amount realized also includes any of your liabil-ities assumed by the Entering party and any liabilities to which the property you sold is subject, such as a mortgage or real estate taxes.

Fair market value. Fair market value is the price at which ownership in the business would be transferred between an Exiting and Entering party, neither being forced to buy or sell, and both having reasonable knowledge of all the facts. This price can be best determined with an independent third-party appraisal.

Amount recognized. A gain or loss realized from a disposition of property is usually recognized as either a gain or loss for tax purposes. Gains resulting from a disposition of property must be included in your gross income. Losses from the disposition of property held for personal use cannot be deducted.

How will a gain be taxed?

As a general rule, the gain on the sale of a business asset will be taxed as ordinary income up to your original basis. Any gain in excess of your original basis may be treated as a capital gain. Here are two examples to illustrate the point:

Example 1: You sell a machine that you used in your business for $900. You had purchased the machine two years and six months ago for $1,000 and had taken depreciation of $500. You would have an ordinary gain of $400 computed as follows:

1. Gross sales price	$ 900
2. Original cost	$1,000
3. Depreciation	500
4. Adjusted basis (2. - 3.)	500
5. Total gain (1. - 4.)	400
6. Total gain plus depreciation (4. + 5.)	900
7. If line 6 is less than line 1. Gain is ordinary	

Example 2: The facts in **Example 2** are the same as in **Example 1** except you sold the machine for $1,100. You would

have an ordinary gain of $500 and a capital gain of $100 computed as follows:

1. Gross sales price	$1,100
2. Original cost	$1,000
3. Depreciation	500
4. Adjusted basis (2. - 3.)	500
5. Total gain (1. - 4.)	600
6. Total gain plus depreciation (4. + 5.)	1,100
7. If line 6. is greater than Line 1. Subtract Line 2 from Line 6. Line 7. is a capital gain	100
8. Subtract Lines 7 From Line 5. Line 8 is an ordinary gain	500

The distinction between ordinary gain and capital gain is an important one. As of this writing, ordinary gain is taxcd at the ordinary income rates, which can currently be as high as 38.6%. Capital gains on the other hand can be taxed at a current rate as low as 8% depending on when the asset was acquired and how long it has been held. You should see your tax advisor to discuss which capital gains rates would apply in your particular situation.

As part of Exiting ownership of your business, there would most likely be intangible assets that would be sold. The following table lists some of the common intangibles sold and whether the Exiting party receives ordinary income or capital gain treatment:

Intangible Asset	Tax Treatment
Unrealized accounts receivable	Ordinary income
Covenant not to compete	Ordinary income
Business books and records, operating systems, or any other information base	Capital gain
Customer lists	Capital gain
Supplier or vendor lists	Capital gain
Any license, permit or other right granted by a governmental unit	Capital gain
Any franchise, trademark or trade name	Capital gain
Workforce in place	Capital gain
Any patent, copyright, formula, process, design, pattern, know how, format or similar item	Capital gain

As of this writing, the installment sales method may be available for certain proprietorships, partnerships and limited liability companies when there is a seller-financed mortgage as part of the transaction. For transfer of ownership to be considered an installment sale there must be at least one payment after the tax year of the sale. For example, if you sell a business in 2002 and receive part of the sales price in 2002 and the remainder after 2002, then the sale is considered an installment sale.

If the exchange of ownership qualifies as an installment sale, then the gain must be reported as an installment sale unless:

1. The Exiting party elects not to use the installment

method, or

2. The Exiting party uses the accrual method of accounting.

Since the area of an installment sale is rather complex, you should see your tax advisor for proper treatment of an installment sale.

Corporations

If your business is incorporated, one of the most important decisions that you must make early on is whether to sell the stock of the corporation or its assets.

In general, Entering parties prefer to purchase assets of the company rather than its stock. By purchasing the assets of the company, the Entering parties insulate themselves from any liabilities that may follow the acquired corporation. Also, by purchasing assets, the Entering party can "step up" the basis of the depreciable assets acquired; whereas, by purchasing the stock of the corporation the current carrying values of the assets remain the same.

Exiting owners generally prefer to sell stock rather than assets. Stock is considered a capital asset. The sale of a capital asset receives better tax treatment than the sale of a non-capital asset. As explained earlier, the sale of a non-capital asset would have ordinary income treatment and maybe partial capital gain treatment; whereas, the sale of a capital asset would have capital gain treatment, which is taxed at lower rates.

Whether a corporation is a C corporation or an S corporation affects how the proceeds will be taxed, when its assets are sold.

For C corporations, the owner could pay twice when the corporation's assets are sold. First there is corporate capital gains tax on any gain from the sale of the assets, and then there is a personal tax on any distribution from the corporation to the owner.

For an S corporation, the proceeds from an asset pass through the corporation to the individual shareholders and retain their tax attributes. For example, long-term capital gains are reported as such on the shareholder's return rather than being lumped in as ordinary income; however, gains associated with business property held for one year or less, inventory, accounts receivable or covenants not to compete are treated as ordinary income.

"With the recent reductions in the long-term capital gains tax rate, more owners of incorporated businesses will push for stock sales when they Exit their business," says Frank A. Gutta, the managing partner of Gutta, Koutoulas & Associates, CPAs in Plantation, Florida. "Although each situation and transaction is different," he says, "in general, Exiting owners want to sell stock and Entering prospects want to buy assets."

Besides the more favorable tax benefits in a stock sale, Exiting owners can also benefit from a stock sale over an asset sale because any business liabilities, whether known or unknown, are transferred to the Entering party via the stock sale. For example, the Entering party in a stock sale could be responsible for unpaid taxes, contract disputes, liabilities arising from employee benefit plans and even future product liability claims. When assets are sold instead of stock, the potential liability problems remain with the Exiting owner. To counteract this argument by the Entering prospect for an asset sale rather than a stock sale, a well-crafted stock sales agreement can exempt the Entering party from any known or unknown liabilities.

As previously stated, another reason for Entering prospects preferring an asset purchase to a stock purchase is that they can "step up" the basis of depreciable assets purchased.

For example, say the Exiting owner purchased some

machinery in 1995 for $6,000 and this machinery has a five-year tax life. In 2002 when the Exiting owner decides to Exit his business, the machinery is fully depreciated and has a net tax value of zero. If the Exiting owner Exits the business in a stock sale, the zero basis of the machinery carriers over to the Entering party, who will not be able to deduct any additional depreciation on this piece of machinery. However, if the machinery were transferred via an asset sale and purchase, then the basis in the machinery would be "stepped up" to its fair market value. If the fair market value of the machine is $5,000, then the Entering owner can start depreciating the machine with a new five-year tax life.

As you can see, in an asset sale it is important for the Exiting owner to know what assets he or she has, where they are and how much they are worth.

Pricing the business tends to be more art than science and several methods could be used for determining the value. It would not be unusual to have two or more respected appraisers arrive at different values for the same business. This is why it is important to use an appraiser with national experience in all of the accepted methods of business appraisal.

Qualified appraisers will normally provide the following:

The **tangible asset value** of the business: $_____
The **intangible asset value** of the business: $_____
The total **fair market value** of the business: $_____

The appraiser generates a price **range**, which represents the highest price an Exiting owner could expect, and the lowest price he/she should accept.

A suggested price is calculated based on the information generated by various formulas, often as many as ten of them.

Sometimes extreme deviations occur and are the product

of formulas, which consider only one or two business factors and are not representative of the total business. The appraiser will make adjustments and allowances for these extremes in the suggested price.

It is important to consider all of the appropriate formulas because to use only one or a few might produce an extreme result. Single "Rules of Thumb" are totally inadequate!

Just because an Exiting owner may encounter negative tax consequences in the Exiting process, an intelligent Entering prospect will not pay more than fair market value for a business. Perceptive Entering prospects will always consider all appropriate formulas and base their decision on their beliefs in all of the factors. Consequently, an Exiting owner should use a *Primary Business Consultant*, appraiser and tax advisor who can prepare them for any eventuality!

As we stated in another chapter, all too often an Exiting business owner completes negotiations only to discover that due to his tax situation he "can't afford to Exit." Sometimes a "creative solution" may be quickly found. More commonly, the tax-bite issue becomes a "dealer-killer" or the anxious owner, afraid he will lose the Entering prospect, concludes he has no choice but to pay. This is not always the case but may instead be the product of bad (or no) advice in a pressure situation.

Avoid this blunder by securing a timely heads up. In thinking through a proposed ownership transfer and your financial objectives, don't focus on expected price alone. Net, net, net is the issue. After getting a professional, third party appraisal, allow your *Primary Business Consultant* to consult an appropriate tax advisor early enough to identity tax strategies that will minimize, defer, or possibly avoid a substantial tax liability. Some require lead-time and specific arrangements in advance of a letter of intent or order to purchase. Others can be addressed during or immediately after negotiations. If there is any doubt about your situation, your *Primary Business*

Consultant will recommend adding the proper professional to your team. In this highly specialized area, the right advisor will add value far beyond the cost of his/her fees, and the wrong one may cost you big time.

In addition to assisting you in the *minimization of tax liabilities* when you Exit business ownership, your *Primary Business Consultant* can additionally consult the proper advisors to assist you in the maximization of investment growth of the proceeds from your Exit of your business. Additionally, allow your trusted coach (*Primary Business Consultant*) to secure the proper advisors to help you in the *minimization of tax liabilities* as you plan for the eventual transfer of these assets to heirs.

THE SEQUENCE OF EVENTS IN AN OWNERSHIP TRANSFER OF PRIVATELY OWNED BUSINESSES

Countless millions of Americans, from the Pilgrims to the pioneers...
have proven that in this unconquerably and justifiably optimistic nation
NOTHING undertaken by free men and free women is impossible.
Robert E. Sherwood

It has been said that with the coordination of a *Primary Business Consultant*, one can put "New smooth sailing freeways on the old road maps of transferring business ownership." This client testimony is the result of many state-of-the-art concepts brought to transactions by these un-compromised business advocates.

To help you understand the many events in Mergers & Acquisitions, we have prepared the following potential list of events in the process of business transfer for which you will want to become familiar. These events are presented in a logical sequence. However, some transactions take on a life of their own and may depart significantly from the sequence of this list.

For this exercise, we will use the sequence we see most often as initiated with a business owner, who for a variety of reasons will be mentally, emotionally and financially prepared to Exit a business. This initiates a possible sequence of:

E^1 - A decision for an owner to Evaluate (appraise) the business
E^3 - An optional "detour" to Enhance (improve) the business before placing it on the market
E^4 - A decision to Exit the business and place it on the market with a *Primary Business Consultant*

E^2 - Negotiations with Entering prospects

E^3 - The new owner should secure an Enhancement Plan to improve the performance, profits and ultimate value of the business

E^1 - Evaluating Business Ownership

The owner should visit the web site **www.ABCbiz.biz** and choose a *Primary Business Consultant* who will be his/her guide through the process of an independent third-party appraisal(s).

<u>Event</u>	<u>Time Table</u>
Make an appointment with a *Primary Business Consultant*.	*5 minutes*
Read chapter 5 in this book and/or "The Guide for Exiting Business Ownership," provided by a *Primary Business Consultant*.	*45 minutes*
Initial visit with *Primary Business Consultant* to discuss the Exit strategy and place an order for one or more of the following:	*1 hour*

- Business Appraisal
- Real Estate Appraisal
- Machinery & Equipment Appraisal
- Environmental Assessment

Completion and delivery of the appraisal(s) and/or assessment(s).	*2-4 weeks*
Visit with the *Primary Business Consultant* and review the appraisal(s).	*1 hour*

Normally the next step is to initiate offering the business in a marketing process with your *Primary Business Consultant,* see **E⁴** below.

E³ Enhancing Business Ownership

Event	Time Table
Read chapter 3 of this book and/or "The Guide for Enhancing Business Ownership," provided by a *Primary Business Consultant.**	*45 minutes*
***Option:** In the event the appraisal(s) does not meet the requirements of the owner, an option can be considered to correct the situation with the initiation of an Enhancement plan (**E³**) with a *Primary Business Consultant.*	*Several months to several years*

E⁴ Exiting Business Ownership

Event	Time Table
Read chapter 5 in this book and/or "The Guide to Exiting Business Ownership," provided by a *Primary Business Consultant.*	*45 minutes*
Enter into an agreement with your *Primary Business Consultant* to administer the marketing process.	*1 hour*
Gathering of information and preparation of marketing materials by the *Primary Business Consultant.*	*2–4 weeks*

Administration of the marketing   *9–12 months*
process by your *Primary Business Consultant*.

Monthly meetings with *Primary Business*   *1 hour*
Consultant to review progress and discuss
plans for future marketing activities.

Consideration of a Letter of Intent and/or   *Varies*
Purchase Agreement through your *Primary*
Business Consultant from an Entering prospect.

Counter Offer period may be required.   *Varies*

Offer accepted with/with out contingencies   *1–3 days*
and earnest money is deposited with Escrow
Closing Attorney

Enter into a specific Purchase Agreement   *Varies*
prepared by Escrow/Closing Attorney.

Process loan provided by owner and/or   *1–6 weeks.*
third party.

Remove contingencies.   *1 week.*

Due-diligence by Entering prospect.   *1–2 weeks.*

Collection and preparation of information to be *Varies*
used in Closing Documents. This will be coordinated by your *Primary Business Consultant*.

Escrow/Closing Attorney prepares closing   *3–7 days*
documents.

Review of Closing Documents with your   *Varies*
Primary Business Consultant and/or
independent attorney.

The Closing...CONGRATULATIONS!   *Varies*

(See **E²** below for a detail explanation of events and time, which may be required by an Entering prospect.)

E⁴ Entering Business Ownership

The prospect for **E**ntering business ownership should visit the web site **www.ABCbiz.biz** to choose a *Primary Business Consultant* and/or a specific business in which they have an initial interest.

Event	Time Table
Make an appointment with a *Primary Business Consultant*.	*5 minutes*
Read chapter 3 in this book and/or "The Guide **E**ntering Business Ownership," provided by a *Primary Business Consultant*.	*45 minutes*
Initial telephone contact with *Primary Business Consultant* to secure a Preliminary Business Profile on business(es) of interest. Execution of a Non-disclosure (confidentiality) form will be required. This can be handled by fax or e-mail.	*15–30 min.*
Initial face-to-face meeting with *Primary Business Consultant* to discuss needs, qualifications and other information on business(es) of interest. Financial statement(s), resume and additional	*1–12 hours*

information will be required. Make a priority choice of a business in which you have prime interest.

Additional meeting(s) to review independent third-party appraisal and additional information provided on the business of prime interest. *1 hour each*

Visit the business with *Primary Business Consultant* and meet the owner(s). Discuss the business with *Primary Business Consultant*. *2 hours*

Develop Letter of Intent/Offer to Purchase and Provide a credit report (or authorization to secure one). *2 hours*

Have *Primary Business Consultant* present offer to owner(s) with an earnest money check made out to the Escrow/Closing Attorney's trust account. *Varies*

Counter offer period may be required. *Varies*

Earnest money deposited with Escrow/ Closing Attorney. *30 minutes*

Enter into a specific Purchase Agreement prepared by an Escrow/Closing Attorney. *Varies*

Process loan provided by owner and/or third-party financing. *1-6 weeks*

Remove contingencies. *1 week*

Due-diligence.   *1–2 weeks*

Primary Business Consultant prepares closing   *3 days*
information for Escrow/Closing Attorney.
Escrow/Closing Attorney prepares closing   *3–7 days*
documents.

Review Closing Documents with *Primary*   *Varies*
Business Consultant* and/or independent attorney.

CLOSING with possession accepted...   *Varies*
CONGRATULATIONS!

Option: In the event the Entering entrepreneur does
not locate an appropriate business to Enter, there
are other options available:

The *Primary Business Consultant* can perform   *4–6 weeks*
a targeted business search for a more suitable
business. This can be a very effective activity.

A start-up business plan can be developed and   *Varies*
monitored by the *Primary Business Consultant*
to assist in the start-up of a new business.

Important: Whatever process is used by the   *Varies*
Entering entrepreneur, he or she should use the
services of the *Primary Business Consultant*
to develop and monitor a Business Enhancement
Plan to maximize the performance, profits and
ultimate value of the business! Read chapter 4
in this book and/or, "The Guide to Business
Enhancement," provided by a *Primary
Business Consultant*.

COMMON MISTAKES IN EVALUATING, ENTERING, ENHANCING & EXITING PRIVATELY OWNED BUSINESSES

Learn from the mistakes of others.
You can't live long enough to make them all yourself.
Author Unknown

I. CONSIDERING AND PURSUING ENTRY INTO BUSINESS OWNERSHIP

Entering Business Ownership for the Wrong Reasons

Owning one's own business is not for everybody. Some realize that too late. They may have made their choice from emotion, perhaps "falling in love" with a "lifestyle business" (for example, a bed & breakfast or a ski resort) without looking at how it would meet basic financial needs. Ego or a desire to project a certain image influenced others. Many acted from desperation: recently unemployed or about to be, they felt a compulsion to "do something" quickly. Wrong reasons and impulsive decisions predictably produce a bad match.

Suggestions: Finding and acting on the right reason requires honest answers to some tough questions: Should I even be considering business ownership? Am I comfortable with risk? Do I possess the essential personal qualities, especially belief in my abilities and myself? What will business ownership do for my goals, and my values that my present situation doesn't allow? What is the right business for me? How will I know? Some answers will be obvious, while others only emerge from an educational process in the effort of trying to find and Enter an established business.

It is imperative to have or develop a high level of self-awareness, and be very realistic about one's own skills, talents

and weaknesses. Sort out true needs from wants and prefer-
ences. Get the perspective of those most immediately affected, such as a spouse. Work with an experienced *Primary
Business Consultant* who will constructively challenge and
focus your thinking, and who is personally committed to
helping you "Enter right." Each new situation will suggest its
own questions, and offer an opportunity to re-think things.
How much do you need to net the first month, the first year?
Can you really go the first six months without taking a
salary? In addition to your financial requirements, is it essential that a good match meet certain lifestyle, geographical,
and other criteria? What must be present for business ownership to be emotionally satisfying? Are you willing, indeed
eager, to do what is required to be successful, even if that
means hard work and long hours? Will you do better in a
structured environment or one less so? Have you managed
people, and do you enjoy it? Do you have sufficient understanding of the business and the industry to be successful?
Are you really looking for a business or trying to "buy a job?"
Don't be afraid of the questions. Hopefully, they are moving
you closer to the right reason(s)for Entering business ownership, and giving clarity to your goals but especially the
requirements of a good match.

Reliance on Compromised or Bad Advice

Those working with an old-style traditional business broker as a customer, and not as a client, often ignore the potential cost of advice or guidance given from *self-serving motives.*
Despite disclosure laws in a number of states, novice purchasers
should not downplay the built-in conflict between their own
interest in Entering ownership of the right business in the right
way (by not overpaying) and the broker's financial stake in a
quick sale and a larger success fee. Also, many unknowingly act
on bad advice given by a trusted professional. This can be every

bit as dangerous and costly. It is particularly difficult to distinguish bad from good advice *at the time it is given*. The distinction is frequently clear only after the fact and from the consequences of the advice. Then, it may be too late to undo the damage. Mistakes commonly come from a client's inexperience and an advisor's lack of professionalism, such as when a professional can't or won't recognize that he is "in over his head" and fails to involve another (or other) professionals who can better serve his/her client's interest. Less obvious is the possible conflict between an Entering client's interest in an appropriate, but cost-effective legal review of a negotiated agreement, and the attorney's practice of "over-lawyering", encouraged by the rewards of increasing billable hours. As a result, a competent attorney, in "protecting his client's interest," may unwittingly cause delays or make "deal-killing" demands that defeat his client's desires and true interest.

Suggestions: Anyone considering and pursuing Entry into business ownership has a need for un-compromised advice and guidance <u>throughout the process</u>. The warning *"caveat emptor"* or Buyer Beware is particularly appropriate here. Protect yourself from what you don't know. Consider engaging a *Primary Business Consultant* to serve as your advocate, committed from beginning to end to assisting you find and Enter the right business in the right way. This experienced professional will be paid for his time and services, based only on what is best for you, his client. Don't allow comfortable relationships or long-term friendships with other professionals to blind you to the critical need for competence, relevant experience, and the integrity to tell you when another professional should be consulted or involved. Your *Primary Business Consultant* can help you assemble a team of professionals and specialists, drawing upon their expertise and advice to advance your goals and interests...whereever that may lead, but in the most cost-effective manner practical.

Going It Alone with a Piecemeal Approach

Many would-be business owners find that their search is more difficult and takes far longer than expected. Typically, they call or meet with every business broker in the city; diligently follow-up with every FSBO listed in the Sunday paper or perhaps, phone some franchisors to get information. Some may send out a number of "if you know about someone …" letters to a limited number of accountants or attorneys in the area. While a few find the right fit, reliance on a self-help program that chases traditional brokers advertised opportunities and is limited to pursuit of only the most obvious candidates is a common mistake. The odds of Entering business ownership this way are indeed long. Less than one in five privately held businesses offered by an Exiting owner or through intermediaries and marketing services is successfully transferred. No wonder so many eventually give up their quest, mistakenly believing that they have done all they could.

Suggestions: An unfocused, partial or slap-dash effort will rarely produce the desired outcome. Success is most likely when the effort is consistent, sustained and part of a comprehensive approach to identify and pursue all relevant options for Entering business ownership. The *Primary Business Consultant* represents a significant alternative to the grossly ineffective traditional approaches. By using his or her services and assistance you can source and explore every conceivable type of Entry opportunity, from established businesses "in the market," to franchises, to those opportunities available in the vast "hidden market" and finally, to consideration of a start-up based on your own vision.

Failing to see "the Forest for the Trees"

As prospective entrepreneurs Evaluate business opportunities they often lose sight of the big picture, miss key relationships, or make flawed assumptions. The net impact of such mistakes is unforeseen (but foreseeable) problems, even possible failure. Inexperienced **E**ntering entrepreneurs focus on historical or current financial performance to the exclusion of factors that impact future profitability, such as changing technology, labor markets or new management itself. Drawn to certain attractive features of a business, they also overlook actual or emergent problems. "Business-as-usual" assumptions that make no allowance for the negative (or positive) impact of an ownership change can be as dangerous as excessively optimistic growth projections that overstate the new owner's abilities as "a miracle worker." Both may result in serious cash flow problems.

Suggestions: Get beyond generalities and superficial impressions. Think in terms of specifics. See things as they are! Do your homework on the business and the industry carefully, frequently asking yourself – "Am I seeing the total picture here?" Do you understand the dynamics of this business, what made it more or less successful, the role that management played? Reality check your understanding of things by drawing on the experience and insights of your professional team led by your *Primary Business Consultant*, and applying worst case/best case scenarios. Be clear about the **E**xiting owner's real responsibilities and true importance to the business. Are you just replacing him or bringing that set of skills necessary for taking the company to the next level? Unless there is good reason for an early departure by the **E**xiting owner, consider negotiating sufficient time to learn the business and reassure all concerned parties. Finally, be conservative in any financial projections. Any third-party lender involved with your project will insist on it. Warning: as you probe for answers to the "right questions" and work through the many issues normally involved, do not fall into the trap of "paralysis of analysis." You must be willing to act decisively on your assumptions or someone else with greater faith in their own abilities and entrepreneurial foresight may take the opportunity away from you.

Paying too much for the Business

Overpaying is the worst fear of most Entering entrepreneurs. It has hard dollar implications for the successful future operation of the business. With few exceptions, the monies committed to the Exiting owner and/or third-party debt service directly reduce that available for working capital or needed capital investment.

Suggestion: Get an independent, third-party appraisal. It will give you a yardstick by which to measure the fairness of any asking price, and guidance. That appraisal should define the core of your negotiating strategy. Also, it should include a "reality check" which is useful in understanding financing options. Engage the most respected appraisal professional you can, one whose experience and quality work will produce immediate credibility with the Exiting owner and his professional advisors. Ask your *Primary Business Consultant* for his recommendation and participation. Finally, don't become involved in a "bidding war" as the danger of overpaying increases dramatically. Know what you can comfortably invest in a business acquisition, taking into account all direct and indirect Entry costs, personal and short-term business needs. Set a spending cap and stay with it.

Ignoring the Two-way Street

Inexperienced Entering entrepreneurs are often their own worst enemies. Many fail to understand that from the first direct contact with an Exiting owner they are being auditioned for the leading role. By saying too much, too little, the wrong thing or by mishandling the request for confidentiality they can alienate the owner, thereby ending any real prospect for Entry into that particular business.

Suggestion: Just showing up and having the dollars is usually not enough. With few exceptions the "right fit" is a matter of critical concern to Exiting owners. When non-financial objectives (such as a future role in the business or fairness to employees, etc.) have equal or greater importance than net proceeds, then the personal qualities and credibility of a successor can become decisive. Your *Primary Business Consultant* sees his role as one of building trust and mutual confidence between the parties. He understands too that in a competitive market situation, prospects need to "sell themselves" to an Exiting owner. At the least this requires a sensitivity and responsiveness to the other party's values and priorities. Personal chemistry can significantly influence an owner's response to your offer, his willingness to extend financing, and the atmosphere during the post-closing transition. Behaviors and communications grounded in recognition that successful transfers require "this two-way street" are more likely to get you in sooner and with fewer problems.

II. ENHANCING YOUR BUSINESS

Too much or too fast, too soon

Frequently, new business owners overreach or get ahead of themselves in actions that produce undesirable consequences. Once in their new business, many initiate changes in policy, personnel, and even organization structure, without a full understanding of what they are doing or the potential impact. Or in anticipation of future growth, they buy extra equipment and incur additional debt long before there is enough demand to justify and pay for the expanded capacity.

Suggestions: Minimally, changes and initiatives should be carefully thought out. Those made impulsively or in a burst of enthusiasm or from superficial analysis are certain to be troublesome in their unintended consequences. Those new at the helm need to recognize that rocking the boat may capsize it. "Steady as she goes" is usually better at first, or until you've gotten comfortable with the currents and crosswinds. Changes, implementing significant change represent a major challenge for management and even experienced, successful business owners. Whether the goal is to improve operations or lay the groundwork for future growth, proceed deliberately and get professional help. All contemplated changes should be part of a comprehensive, long-range plan that anticipates your eventual and inevitable Exit from business ownership. Consistent use of a *Primary Business Consultant* will significantly enhance current profits and future value!

Too Busy Fighting Off the Gators to Drain the Swamp

Without doubt, this colorful expression points out the most common mistake of business ownership, the excessive preoccupation with "the here and now" to the virtual exclusion of the future. It has been expressed many ways: crisis management; dealing with the symptoms, not the causes; responding to the urgent vs. the important, etc. The "gators" appear in many forms: chronic personnel turnover, cash-flow problems, quality or service issues, burnout, competitive pressures, no time any more for the family, shrinking market share, regulatory compliance headaches.... "Damn, this is no fun any more." The not-so-funny thing is that for too many business owners the gators are always there, maybe more of 'em, and they'll never have time to drain the swamp.

Suggestions: Step back and catch your breath. Ask yourself: "Why am I doing this?" "Why did I get into to business?" "What were my dreams, my vision, goals?" "What has happened to them?" "What is important to me, today?" "What of the future?" "Where will this company be in five, ten, fifteen years or more?" "Where will I be?" If you had a plan, long-term, mid-term, short-term, revisit and update. If you don't, get one…get serious about the future. Get help and drain the swamp! Don't make the mistake of thinking you can do it all.

If you are a results-driven business owner consider engaging a *Primary Business Consultant*. He or she can work with you <u>and</u> for you, offering un-compromised advice and accountability for developing and implementing programs, making changes with maximum short-term and long-term impacts and benefit. A *Primary Business Consultant* will actively help you increase production and/or profits almost immediately. He or she can help you recover or find for the first time the excitement and satisfactions of business ownership through changes that reduce the stresses and frustrations from whatever source(s). A *Primary Business Consultant* can also help you create or revise/update your roadmap to the future and show you how to maximize the long-term value of your business and how you can recapture that fuller value when you finally Exit business ownership.

III. EXITING BUSINESS OWNERSHIP

Flying Blind

Many owners "fly blind" at this most critical time in their business career. Their approach to the multiple decisions involved with a business transfer is largely improvised and reactive. Unrealistic assumptions, wishful thinking and emotionalism dangerously influence their actions. No planning, poor planning and inadequate preparation <u>are the most common and fundamental</u> mistakes Exiting owners make. A few business owners start thinking about their Exit at the very time they Enter business, and run their companies with an eye to that inevitable day. Others managed enough planning and preparation later to come out fairly well or get something they can live with. It is a certainty that most never knew how much better they could have done. But for many owners "too little, too late" became a "no sale" situation, the defeat of their goals, and bitter disappointment.

Suggestions: A truly successful transfer of business ownership starts with a plan, followed by appropriate preparation. How much planning and with what lead-time depends on so many factors that is impossible to prescribe for all owner situations and businesses. What has been said bears repeating: good planning and preparation is fundamental, and further, that while it's never too early to begin, it can be too late to make a difference. Take the better option and ask your *Primary Business Consultant* to help you start developing your Exit strategy as soon as you Enter business ownership. In addition to the time needed to define and refine strategic direction as it relates to Exiting your business, optimal outcomes require time to complete proper preparations. These can include cleaning up the balance sheet, settling outstanding litigation, addressing environmental or regulatory issues that might become "deal killers," negotiating leases, and disposing of excess assets. Proper preparation always includes an independent business appraisal, and often equipment and machinery and/or real property appraisals.

Going it alone or on bad advice

Granted some owners, either with the active assistance of their attorney and CPA, or primarily by their own effort, succeed, sometimes with acceptable, but rarely optimal, results. More do not, or end up with a "failed sale" (a completed transaction involving a business that later has to be taken back by the original owner). For most Exiting entrepreneurs the transfer of business ownership is a one-time experience. Considering the tremendous monetary and lifestyle consequences that it has for both the owner and family members the need to "get it right" should be obvious. Unless one is willing to accept the costs of a potential, possibly expensive mistake, it would be wise to recall the old saying, " A lawyer who represents himself has a fool for a client." Even when the limitations and risks of self-help are recognized, and the Exiting entrepreneur decides to rely on professionals, success isn't assured. Costly, hard-dollar mistakes, and occasionally, outright failure, can be traced to some owner's inability to distinguish good advise from bad, ethical professionals from self-servers, and even an unwillingness to value and bear the cost of help that can make all the difference.

Suggestion: Good, timely professional advice concerning current or future tax liabilities, avoidance of potential litigation, or negotiating the "best deal"- fair for all parties (thereby minimizing the risk of a failed sale), can save the Exiting entrepreneur many thousands of dollars over the fees that will be paid. While success is most easily measured in hard dollars, there are also the less tangible benefits of peace of mind, a stable and lasting transfer to the "right party," fairness to loyal employees, a timely transition to an alternative future, and the avoidance of future litigation. These often are of greater importance.

Successful transfers depend on how well the owner's team understands the necessity of managing a complex process where the "devil is in the detail" through honest communications and credible information, keeping things moving forward, and curbing the destructive potential of emotionalism. If you are to be successful, and realize your optimal objectives, personally and financial, you must be the one in control of the process. Put together the best team possible. If you haven't already, consider the services of an *Primary Business Consultant* who will not allow himself/herself to be put in a situation where a conflict of interest is possible, whose proven ability to work successfully with other professional advisors and understanding of the "big picture" will serve you well. Choose one who will represent you specifically in this process and most

115

importantly will be your strongest advocate, assuring that you remain in control. Review the professional competencies and <u>relevant</u> experience of team members. Minimally, include also an involved accountant with strength in the tax area and a transaction attorney. Don't make the mistake of relying <u>exclusively</u> on a trusted professional who doesn't have either the experience, skills or temperament you need but who may hesitate to admit it because of your friendship. The true professional guided by his code of ethics will excuse himself or involve another when he believes he can't serve your best interest.

Exiting for the wrong reason(s), no good reason or impulsively

"False starts" occur in situations when an owner goes to market prematurely or otherwise acts to transfer business ownership but is not really ready personally or emotionally. Even if the effort succeeds, it may be inconsistent with the owner's best interests, and rarely will produce optimal results.

When Exiting a business is seen as the <u>only</u> solution to chronic frustrations, financial distress, and "problems" that could have been handled by specific operational, personnel, or financial changes, then Exiting may be for the wrong reason. Commonly, the owner will concede that if this or that were "fixed" he'd keep the business, or stay on in a different role with a new owner. Whether from desperation or bad advice, some go ahead anyway, and learn first hand there is no market for "buying the other guy's problems", at least for their price. Many owners may not realize that a *Primary Business Consultant* can help them deal successfully with the frustrations or poor financial performance, and at the same time build additional value for the business well in excess of the cost of such assistance.

Business owners in the market for "no good reason" also illustrate the "false start." Lacking real motivation they wait for a "greater fool" to come along and pay an outrageous price, wasting everyone's time, including their own. Finally, there is the entrepreneur who impulsively reacts to the approach of a suitor or industry consolidator. Driven by emotion, ego or fearful an apparent "window of opportunity" will close; he'll buy into someone else's "instant Exit plan," realizing later that it wasn't what he really wanted. If properly prepared, one can take advantage of unexpected opportunities to achieve personal and business goals. If not, playing in the other guy's game, primarily in a reactive way, usually proves costly.

Suggestions: Predictably the first question a prospective Entering entrepreneur will ask an Exiting owner is not "what do you want for your business" but "why are you Exiting?" You need a credible reason! Be absolutely clear as to what you want to accomplish. This will reduce the dangers of emotionalism or wishful thinking, and "false starts." Focus on your objectives- personal and financial, near-term and longer range. Explore alternatives, getting the best professional advice. Recognize that Exiting will almost never make financial sense since most entrepreneurs could receive in approximately three to five years of annual earnings what they would net from the Exit of the business, but still own it!!! If you are going to follow through an Exit strategy to completion, be sure there is motivation stronger than just putting some money in your pocket. Without it, you may find at the time of final commitment that you are emotionally unable to consummate the transaction. Some obvious and compelling motivations are:

- Retirement
- Serious Illness
- Divorce
- Disability of the Owner Operator
- Death of the Owner Operator
- Burnout of the Owner Operator
- Desire to Upgrade One's Status or Profession

- "Grass is Greener"…the allure of a new challenge or "Just having to try something different"
- Pursuit of a Better Investment Strategy…leveraging into something bigger or more promising.
- Inadequate borrowing capabilities
- Ending One's Financial and Legal Exposure to Risk/ Risk Reduction

While this is not an exhaustive list, it suggests the variety of motivators that can validate and drive a commitment to Exiting business ownership. They will require honest answers to some basic questions: *How strong* is my need for a redefined future: retirement, a new challenge, ending my exposure to risk, gifting to heirs or a favorite charity, etc.? Have I reached the point where I can commit to this course *with no turning back? Am I mentally ready?* Where you have mixed feelings about going forward, talk to others who have been through the process, and you'll find this is normal. For some entrepreneurs, determining "owner readiness" is fairly simple. For others, a more structured and lengthy process of succession planning or Exit planning will be appropriate. Through this the entrepreneur will focus and refine his or her priorities, and with expert guidance look at the feasibility of transferring the business to "insiders" (family members, employees, management, etc.), before any decision to "go outside." In the final analysis there should be a credible, personal or emotionally grounded reason for doing it, and a clear understanding of the desired outcomes.

Not Knowing the Market Value of your Business

Not knowing what your business is worth means not knowing if a contemplated transfer can meet all your financial objectives. That makes it impossible to determine if the timing is right for you. Should you press ahead anyway when reacting to a suitor's approach you are vulnerable in another regard. Without a benchmark or yardstick, how can you evaluate the fairness of *any* offer? You can't!!! Ignorance of current market value is costly in other ways. An Exiting entrepreneur may unknowingly under-price his company, potentially leaving significant dollars on the table. Or, unknowingly pricing your business too high will "blow away" qualified Entering prospects, prolonging market exposure, increasing the likelihood of a breach of confidentiality. Along with a "take- it or-leave-it" attitude, gross overpricing can totally defeat an entrepreneur's goals. It is one reason why a number of businesses never transfer, and are closed down with the assets liquidated for pennies on the dollar.

Suggestions: Getting an appraisal by an independent, experienced, third-party professional is an essential, first planning step. This is the only way to determine "business readiness" or whether the business is likely to command the price, and produce the proceeds the Exiting entrepreneur needs. Most importantly, going through the appraisal process usually fosters a more realistic attitude toward price, thereby eliminating or minimizing unrealistic expectations, traditionally a major obstacle to successfully Exiting business ownership. Since there will be many options for securing a business appraisal, do so as an informed consumer. Use an independent, third-party. Experience shows that a formal opinion of value from a respected, independent third-party puts <u>you in control</u>, allowing you to drive the process from your own point of view. The key is the credibility of the appraiser, and indeed of all information shared with interested parties and their professional advisors. A good appraisal should also include a "sanity check" which will establish or not its financiability. Consider too whether the appraiser and his work will be able to withstand a court challenge, in the unlikely event that might occur.

Failing to Consider the Tax Consequences of a Contemplated Transfer

All too often an Exiting entrepreneur completes negotiations only to discover that due to his tax situation he "can't afford to Exit." Sometimes a "creative solution" may be quickly found. More commonly, the tax-bite issue becomes a "deal-killer" or the anxious owner, afraid he will lose the Entering entrepreneur, concludes he has no choice but to pay. This is not always the case but may instead be the product of bad advice in a pressure situation.

Suggestions: Avoid this blunder by giving your tax advisors a timely heads up. In thinking through a proposed transfer and your financial objectives, don't focus on expected price alone. Net, net, net is the issue. After getting a professional, third-party appraisal, allow your *Primary Business Consultant* to consult a CPA or tax advisor early enough to identify tax strategies that will minimize, defer, or possibly avoid a substantial tax liability. Some require lead-time and specific arrangements well in advance of a letter of intent or offer. Others can be addressed during or immediately after negotiations. If there is any doubt whether your tax advisor can provide the needed expertise, ask your *Primary Business Consultant* whom he would recommend adding to your team. In this highly specialized area, the right advisor will add value far beyond the cost of his or her professional fees, and the wrong one may cost you big time. Just remember –"you delay, you pay."

Warning: If, after an appraisal and tax planning, it is evident that the anticipated net proceeds won't meet the Exiting owner's financial needs, do not make the mistake of adjusting up the offering price of the business. Recognize that what a business is worth (as measured by its correctly appraised value) and what an Exiting owner needs financially are totally independent variables. If they should coincide, that fact will establish business readiness. Often, they do not! Rather than putting the business on the market at an unrealistically, high price (to satisfy the needs), engage the services of a *Primary Business Consultant* to legitimately increase the value of the business over the required period of time.

Failing to Anticipate and Properly Respond to an Entering Prospect's Need for Information.

Poor preparation shows up in many ways. Information that is dated, incomplete, or unexplained often leaves a prospect frustrated. Evasive answers, delays in producing information, and especially "unpleasant surprises" from current financial statements call into question the owner's good faith. Too much "bad stuff" will discourage interested parties from pursuing an opportunity.

Suggestions: All prospective Entering entrepreneurs need certain information to qualify their own interest and determine if the business is a fit with their objectives. An Exiting owner's credibility is enhanced, sustained, diminished, even destroyed by his communications, by the information given, by his responsiveness from the beginning of the process to the end. Prepare first by giving careful thought to *what information* you will share *with whom and when*. Then, get it all together, and have it ready. Finally, get it right. Use correct and current information. Your *Primary Business Consultant* will know the core information needs and how best to format these, while safeguarding confidentiality. He or she will orchestrate the timely flow of critical information to keep the process moving forward. It is essential to "tell your story," and preparation is the key whether using a Preliminary Profile or a Full Profile. The objective of a Preliminary Profile is to stimulate interest in the opportunity and make it easier for a qualified party to determine his next step and the need for a Full Profile. Together, they must communicate what is included, the specifics of your pre-negotiating position, the basics of the opportunity and benefits of this purchase. Anticipating a serious party's legitimate need for information does not require that you open up everything after a 'tight' Non-Disclosure Agreement is signed or the first face-to-face. Extremely sensitive and proprietary information should be shared only in the due diligence phase, after the Entering entrepreneur indicates further seriousness with a Letter of Intent. Remember, "It's not over 'til it's over" and even customer data can be shared in safe formats.

Going Nowhere with Inappropriate Prospects or Just Waiting for Something to Happen

Owners attempting to Exit their businesses, using business marketing companies or traditional business brokers waste a great deal of time chasing or being chased by "tire-kickers." These are financially and motivationally unqualified, and even curious competitors - some more interested in trade secrets than in consummating a transaction. Practitioners of traditional approaches try to make "something happen" by working "a numbers game" and may get lax in qualifying suspects. Consequently, some clients experience so much activity that it must seem as if they have been caught in " a revolving door." In contrast, other clients, motivated owners of fairly priced, but hard-to-sell businesses, anxiously wait (and wait) for any indication of interest.

Although business ownership has been, and continues to be transferred this way, the odds are far longer than they are made to appear in claims, actual or implied. Knowledgeable industry professionals long ago described these traditional approaches as "a Las Vegas gamble," because so few clients win big and most do not win at all. SBA statistics and business brokerage trade publications accept that upwards of 4 out of 5 attempted transfers aren't successful. Lack of focus (shotgunning the market) and almost exclusive reliance on a single tool (newspaper advertising or video packages sent into a national market) with little or no follow-up account, in part, for this dismal record. Beyond the formula little is done, certainly nothing proactively or very creative. (Other characteristic weaknesses are identified below).

Suggestions: Marketing plays at least as significant a role in the successful transfer of business ownership to third parties as it does in the successful sale of any other product or service. Become informed about your marketing options. Look hard at the different approaches and different service providers. Find out how prospects are qualified. Don't be seduced by claims, ask about the record, then make an informed selection as to which is most likely to get the results required by your financial and emotional goals. If you have already engaged someone but are disappointed, seek alternatives for future action, while honoring any contractual commitments you presently have.

What should you look for? A well-conceived marketing plan will have focus and creativity, the "missing pieces" of traditional approaches. It must be comprehensive in design, yet target sources most likely to produce appropriate prospects. The individual, corporate, or equity group who is the "best prospect" is the one who can meet all or the most important of the exiting owner's goals. There usually are several parties capable of playing that role and frequently, they are found in the not-so-obvious places. Start by identifying various groups and/or types of individuals based on a careful review of possible operational, market niche, location or other types of matches. *Primary Business Consultant*s not only have the soundest approach but the experience and successes that validate it. Understandably, exiting owners often become over anxious and impatient for results. However, to find the better match, one needs to allow enough time for the process to work.

Negotiating with Only One Prospect at a Time or Just Cooling Your Heels

When an Exiting owner gets emotionally invested in a single party, pursuing one prospect at almost any cost, he or she is dangerously close to giving away control of the process at a most critical time. The mistake of losing the probable leverage of competitive offers is implied in this warning – "If you have only one prospect, you have no prospect, the prospect has you." While this risk is real, negotiating this <u>way by choice</u> need not turn out <u>badly</u>, if the Exiting entrepreneur remains disciplined, recalls his optimal objectives, bargains hard but fairly, and sticks with deadlines. Retaining control in this situation becomes very difficult unless backstopped by a marketing plan that is consistently implemented to bring forward qualified prospects. Indeed, *the ideal* is to create the conditions for a controlled auction precisely because having and using the leverage is thought to be in the client's interest.

What is obviously <u>not</u> in the client's interest is the situation where there is little possibility of leverage. The Exiting owner just waits for something to happen because his professional representative doesn't know what to do, or if he did, wouldn't <u>do all that was needed</u> because he couldn't afford the "extra efforts" or didn't have a great enough incentive. That describes many old-style brokers working for a contingent success fee. Self-interest and economic survival dictates that they concentrate their time and limited resources on the "doable deals" (usually high-demand, often under priced businesses), while treating the difficult-to-sell as "throw-a-ways" or neglecting them entirely. Unknowingly many Exiting owners have participated in this "Las Vegas gamble" only to be deeply disappointed with the outcome.

Suggestions: The successful third-party transfer of business ownership and achievement of optimal objectives generally *requires a consistent, pro-active and actual "best effort," wherever it may lead.* A *Primary Business Consultant* can meet your need for results through a professional, business-like approach. He or she will be an un-compromised advocate of your interests, committed to using proven marketing tools to get results, bringing forward fifty or more new ideas when others don't work, and willingly accountable by means of timely communication, scheduled monthly reviews, and documented efforts. While it costs no more than if you attempted to do all the necessary things yourself or if you took the Las Vegas gamble, be assured that all that needs to be done will indeed be done as quickly as possible…and that you, the client, will remain in control throughout.

Although it is desirable to have several Entering entrepreneurs competing vigorously for your business, a reality check suggests this often will not happen. Practically speaking, you cannot make an interested prospect wait very long while you try to bring others to the negotiating table. You need to take them as they come, treating each as if he or she was the only one. Recently, an attractive and properly priced offering drew many prospects for an initial look but all walked away without any offers. The Exiting owner never panicked because he was using the services of a *Primary Business Consultant* with over fifty marketing resources and was receiving monthly reports of the various efforts to attract prospects. Eventually, the right one made a full-priced offer (which was the only offer), and the transaction was consummated in short order. The obvious lesson is to treat every prospect as if he or she was the only one, for indeed they may be! Remember too that flexibility rooted in recognition of the need for a "win-win" between all parties and timely responses are usually essential ingredients of successful outcomes. Conversely, trying to dominate in negotiations and excessive and unjustifiable delaying are simply counter-productive.

Making Promises You Cannot Keep and Requirements that are Unrealistic

Some Exiting owners have learned that what is personally important to them can produce unrealistic expectations of what an Entering prospect will accept. Out of a genuine concern for loyal employees, suppliers, and/or customers who have played a significant role in building and maintaining the business, they have insisted that relationships be maintained or new ones formalized with these important but secondary parties only to find that this hindered, even threatened a proposed transaction.

Suggestions: It matters not that an Exiting owner is well motivated or that the maintenance of such relationships is a requirement (indeed a necessity) for the Entering entity! Inappropriate promises and unrealistic requirements generally produce unnecessary complications. They may even become a "deal killer." How? Premature notification to and involvement of secondary parties risk the loss of confidentiality and control over the process. It not only restricts the ability of the Entering entity to make changes in these relationships, when such are necessary to improve financial performance, but creates a situation where a potential transaction can be held hostage by the unreasonable demands of a secondary player. Unless preservation of certain relationships is a "non-negotiable" item for the Exiting owner, it is generally best to put a premium on confidentiality and allow the Entering entity to negotiate its own terms with all secondary parties.

Neglecting the Business

Some Exiting entrepreneurs become so preoccupied with the details of the transfer process, their post-transfer future, or allow themselves to be distracted by the emotional roller coaster of courtship, and negotiation, that "no one is minding the store." Should neglect produce a noticeable, negative impact on financial performance, expect some hard questions, and don't be surprised if an Entering entrepreneur wants to renegotiate or backs away entirely.

Suggestions: This critical phase of your business career is not the time to drift or coast. Remember the importance that current information and credibility has for those seriously interested. Stay focused on the present, and on your business and goals. Do not neglect your customers, suppliers, employees, and the general operation of the business during the process. The right team of professional advisors under the leadership of your *Primary Business Consultant* will buffer you from the many distractions and temptations, while keeping you informed and involved at the appropriate times. In reality, during the year of implementing an Exit strategy, you need to give your business your most intense interest, working harder and smarter than during any other year of ownership.

Becoming Impatient

One of the most asked questions regarding Exiting business ownership is: " How long will it take?" Not surprisingly, there is no pat answer. While some transactions have been consummated in one to two months, others have taken well over a year. On average it can take one to three months to complete an independent, third party appraisal. Another month or more may be required to determine the real objectives of the Exiting owner and design a customized plan. It can then take three to nine months to locate the appropriate Entering entrepreneur and negotiate the terms of the transaction. Figure another month or two months for getting through the due diligence phase and closing the transaction.

Suggestions: As you can see, a full year can be consumed in a properly managed ownership transfer. There is no uniform timetable for all businesses. If you are truly committed to an optimal outcome, and securing the ultimate rewards of your years of hard work, planning and preparation for this inevitable passage, then you will understand the need to be patient and allow for whatever is required in your particular situation to properly mature and bear fruit.

THE BOTTOM LINE...
YOUR SUCCESS IS YOUR CHOICE!

A man is not a failure, no matter how many
times he fails, unless, and until, he begins to
blame somebody else for it.
Author Unknown

As a student in high school I received good advice from some of the best mentors I have known. One told me: "When things get tough, improve your personal skills and work harder...that is about all you can do." He encouraged me to go to college and thereby begin a life-long commitment to improving skills. One of our associates calls this "Life-Long Learning." The counsel of another came later when he said: "Your success will depend directly on the choices you make and for which you take total responsibility."

Using the example of unsuccessful attorneys who attend the same law school as one who became a United States Supreme Court Justice, a college mentor illustrated a point confirmed repeatedly by experience: those attending (graduating) college, university and professional schools not only don't achieve at the same level, but are not even assured of success. After two university degrees, several professional certifications and licenses, and over three decades of experience with business owners in various industries, I am convinced he was right.

What accounts for the difference in levels of personal achievement? Many capable, talented individuals attend institutions of higher learning, secure certifications and licenses, gain a lot of practical experience, and yet never achieve significant success.

Why? The answer is not that they didn't work hard (or hard enough), and smarter in many cases. More importantly, some failed to make intelligent choices in the application of this training and experience. They may not have chosen wisely those with whom/for whom they worked or failed to recognize how essential it is to create a team built on trust, integrity and mutual respect.

Many entrepreneurs work harder and smarter but with varying results/degrees of accomplishment. While both of these qualities are necessary, significant success requires something more! <u>The success of an entrepreneur depends on consistency in making the right choices and taking total responsibility for them over the course of one's business career.</u>

One of my high-school mentors impressed upon me the importance of taking total responsibility for my choices in a way I will never forget. Mr. Hancock owned the finest clothing store in our small East Texas town where I worked after school. During one of his semi-annual 1/2 price sales, I mistakenly sold a suit that did not have attached to it a red 1/2 price tag.

After my customer left the store with his new suit and a smile on his face, Mr. Hancock asked to see the sales ticket to which I should have attached the red 1/2 price tag. Being a smart high school student with a quick mind and sharp wit, I began immediately to share with him some hurriedly composed excuses for my costly mistake.

My less than impressed mentor stopped me abruptly, demanding that I repeat after him the following:

Mr. Hancock: "I"

Me: "I"

Mr. Hancock: "Messed" (I think he might have used another word)

Me: "Messed"

Mr. Hancock: "Up!"

Me: "Up!"

After this exchange, he admonished me to work a little "smarter" with future customers and to "take full responsibility" for my mistakes, or I would be "looking for other employment." I remember this experience every time someone tries to convince me that their lack of success comes from reasons other than their failure to make the right choices and take total responsibility for them.

Over the years I have experienced a lot of "Mr. Hancocks" who have shared similar qualities of leadership that have been very helpful to me. These qualities combined with the challenge of making the right choices could consume more pages than are available in this short chapter. Consequently, let's look only at a selected number of these street-savvy choices every entrepreneur should recognize and consider in Evaluating, Entering, Enhancing, and Exiting business ownership.

What follows are my "top ten" from the many choices you may need to make over the course of your business ownership cycle. Hopefully, these will help to mega-size your success!

(1) Recognize that when you are not in control, someone else is controlling you.   Choose to take control of anything that significantly affects you!

Become a decision maker so you don't have to follow the initiative of someone else. You are the only one responsible for your destiny. Imagine and embark on a mission that can create an energy and passion within you. Then never allow anyone to take it away from you.

(2) Don't be a dictator. Choose to be a leader, an exemplary and set yourself apart from the crowd.

To inspire, a good leader should become unique among his/her peers and an example of high performance.

The ability to be sensitive and gracefully/easily accept constructive criticism breeds the acceptance of criticism in those you lead. This creates the trust necessary for teamwork. Become able to show sincere empathy.

Develop the ability to timely and accurately assess incidents that confuse others. This skill will give you the opportunity to implement your own ideas.

Another lesson I learned in high school was that it was no fun on the bus going home after a game lost. The real excitement was on the winning bus. Be a winning example. Through your own resolve and commitment, challenge winners to follow you. With this attitude and example you create a life of excitement for all concerned.

(3) Make the choice that honesty is not only the best policy; it is the only policy!

The only way you can expect total honesty from others is to accept no less from yourself. Follow the highest ethical standards, which produce the best for all involved, including but not limited to greater financial success.

Morals are beliefs, and that's good. Ethics are actions, and that's better. Some religious groups teach that practicing higher ethics is not easy, which requires sacrifice. I don't accept this at all! Once you understand that good ethics creates good and bad ethics creates bad, the choice becomes obvious. The truth is higher ethics produce greater success. Where's the problem?

(4) If you cannot win the war, don't choose to get into it!

Get on the leading edge of your industry by developing the ability to consistently outperform your competitors. You accomplish this with your leading-edge concepts and higher performance. You don't have time to play at every game, so choose to play the ones you can win. If the best you can project is second or third place, then choose another game in which you can ultimately place first.

How do you decide to "go to war?" First, decide if the

undertaking is worth the cost. Next, determine if you have the necessary/required resources available. Third, select the proper personnel and give them the authority, support and finances required. Fourth, make them accountable and monitor their progress to assure completion in a timely manner.

I recently observed the behavior of an association board of directors whose pursuit of a very worthy goal ended in miserable failure. Upon reflection as to cause of their disaster, I concluded they violated every one of the four principles.

(5) Change before you are forced to do so.

Change first and everyone else will follow you. If they change first, you will be following them. Either take a calculated risk and start progress or you will be forced to follow someone who did. It has often been said that the "only thing constant in life is change." If you want to be in charge, change first.

Be aware and prepared for economic change before it is forced on you. Healthy profits come from leaner operations. Be proactive in necessary cash flow changes. Make a more profitable use of expenses so you won't have to cut them. If necessary expenses are making money for you, be willing to increase them as long as the benefits significantly exceed the cost. In other words, build muscle and you won't have to worry about trimming the fat.

(6) Make the choice to admit reality.

Forget the past, and be honest about current reality concerning strengths and weaknesses, what needs to be changed and what retained. Be especially sensitive to the need for profitability. Do not do anything that is not profitable. If you must temporarily deal with an undesirable reality, always visualize a successful outcome. What appears to be a defeat is never permanent unless you allow it to be. Consider setbacks and identified weaknesses as temporary pauses for reorganization, opportunities to reorder priorities and refocus one's thinking.

(7) Make good choices for good physical, emotional, and spiritual health.

I am impressed and inspired by those who reach high standards of performance in spite of handicaps. Plan and act on proven principles that maintain good physical and emotional health. You will be able to do more for yourself and others. Make your health as much a passion as your financial goals.

(8) Attitudes come free, so choose a great one, but prepare to pay the price to sustain it!

Authentic attitudes are reflections of good values. Fake attitudes become transparent and obvious to discerning individuals. Nothing can replace integrity and accountability. Express and embody your attitude with appropriate and consistent behavior.

Not only must you have a great attitude, you must choose to surround yourself only with those individuals who have made successful attitude choices. Refine your requirement to make excellent personnel choices. Just as important, you must be willing to remove or reassign them in a timely manner when it becomes obvious they cannot meet attitude and performance requirements.

Choose wisely your clients and/or customers. Your attitude, level of income and lifestyle will soon become a reflection of those you have chosen for clients.

A good sense of humor is indispensable. Learn to laugh at yourself. A simple mistake is not the end of the world unless you make it repeatedly. The first time you should just fix it, laugh and learn from it.

(9) Choose to work all day!

My wife and I are in the process of building a home/office/training center in the Colorado mountains. The inability to find workers, who will work every day, and all day, has become a real obstacle to accomplishing our goal in a timely manner. In this rural setting, you soon become realistic that many workers have chosen to live "hand to mouth" earning just enough for groceries and liquor for the week. They often return to work only when they are out of groceries and liquor...and, not necessarily always in that order of priority. Most successful entrepreneurs understand they must show up every day, and, work all day.

You should develop the ability to know the difference between being busy and being productive. Check up on yourself and others with systematic (and honest) "goal tending." Put your goals into a screen saver on your computer monitor. This will allow you to constantly assess your activities by their contributions to your goals, rather than just filling up the day.

Once you are committing all of your time to productive activities, you can use your imagination to set bigger goals which are more challenging and rewarding. Work then becomes fun and builds muscle for success...busy is just boring.

(10) Choose to reward yourself, as well as those who have chosen to help you!

Success is about rewarding yourself upon honest achievement, not always taking from yourself to the point that you dislike what you've created.

Perhaps more importantly, it is about giving to those who helped you achieve instead of withholding from them. Your success is guaranteed when you have helped those around you become successful.

The best reward you can give to those working with you is to help them develop their skills and talents to the fullest. A great leader is at his/her best when they have developed others to perform at a level equal to their own. Once you have built a great team around you, inspire them to a level above your own. This shows that you care about them as individuals, not just performers.

I recently saw a slogan on a truck of a large grocery chain that claimed "our people make the difference." This is true, and, to keep them making the difference, they must be inspired to reach greater challenges, and be rewarded at a level equal to their performance.

History has many examples of great leaders who were strongly committed to and driven by these tangible and intangible values. Your success depends upon your commitment to both.

THE BOTTOM LINE...*YOUR $UCCESS IS YOUR CHOICE!*